SOLVING THE BUSINESS PUZZLE

SOLVING THE BUSINESS PUZZLE

Gill Fielding

Published by New Generation Publishing in 2022

Copyright © Gill Fielding 2022

First Edition

The author asserts the moral right under the Copyright, Designs and Patents Act 1988 to be identified as the author of this work.

All Rights reserved. No part of this publication may be reproduced, stored in a retrieval system or transmitted, in any form or by any means without the prior consent of the author, nor be otherwise circulated in any form of binding or cover other than that which it is published and without a similar condition being imposed on the subsequent purchaser.

Paperback: 978-1-80031-218-0
Hardback: 978-1-80031-217-3
Ebook: 978-1-80031-216-6

www.newgeneration-publishing.com

New Generation Publishing

This book is dedicated, with huge thanks, to my business partner, Louise Thorpe, who has the ability to take my random and often chaotic thoughts and turn them into business reality.

I would also like to thank all the Devon-based staff at Fielding Financial, and particularly the magnificent marketing department, who have contributed to this book in the areas where their expertise was, frankly, greater than mine.

Huge thanks also go to Debbie Franklin who made such a massive contribution to the reporting section.

Finally, I would like to express my appreciation to all the contributors who have interspersed this text with their own version of their business reality. We learn more from watching others succeed and fail than we can from any textbook. There is a full list of these contributors at the back of this book so please go and look them up, see what they do and then follow their journeys.

Contents

STARTING BLOCKS	1
Introduction	2
What the heck: why are we doing this?	5
The overall business growth structure	9
THE SALES FUNNEL	22
A. Marketing	26
B. Sales	68
C. After the Sale	107
D. Social Media and the Virtual World	112
PROCESS	138
A. The systemisation process	139
B. The people (and their processes)	159
REPORTING	185
Part One: MIS and KPIs	188
Part Two: Formal reporting	207
LEADERSHIP	237
A. Leading the people: Introduction	238
B. Business leadership	251

FINISHING BLOCKS 256

Appendix: Marketing Acronyms 260
Contributors 263

STARTING BLOCKS

Introduction

There is no magic formula or magic bullet for business success. Most businesses fail – apparently – although I suspect the failure rate depends on the definition of failure, the type of business, and the type of business owner.

Size or profile is no guarantee of success. Of the top companies selected by Tom Peters for his book: 'In Search of Excellence', there were some pretty large and influential companies that subsequently failed: Wang, Atari and Kmart. If we look wider at the Fortune 500 companies in the US: only 12% of the companies listed in 1955 were still in business in 2014, and slightly less than half - 49 – of the FTSE 100 companies in existence in 1999 were still trading in 2015.

When we look at smaller companies, the SMEs (Small to Medium Enterprises) we're told that 9 out of 10 startups fail but that's wildly pessimistic. Figures from the US suggest that 80% make it through the first year and 30% make it to ten years in businesses, but that still means that 70% don't make the decade.

And yet there are about 650,000 new companies formed in the UK each year and almost as many formed per MONTH in the USA where there are almost **28 million small businesses,** of which 22 million are self-employed with no additional employees (called non-employers). Across America, there are approximately 160 million people in work, **over 50%** of which **work in small businesses which** have generated over **65% of the net new jobs** since 1995, and over half of all small businesses (52%) are run from home.

In the UK the working population is about 32 million and there are about 5.7 million SMEs (as at the time of writing) who accounted for 99.9% of all private sector business in the UK. SMEs employed over 16 million people and generated 51% of all private sector turnover in the UK.

Wherever you live in the world starting, owning or running your own business is a big issue: the small and medium-sized organisations make up the majority of the major world economies, and yet very few of us actually get any guidance or education to help. This is partly because we *are* millions of small businesses and there is no 'one size fits all' approach to what we do.

Knowing how significant small businesses are to the overall economy, Governments would love to encourage and support them, but it's a tough task to reach several million individuals scattered business owners all sitting in their individual shop, or office or home doing their own thing. It's a lot easier for governments to find, reach and consequently support larger organisations where there are organised workforces and often several hundred or even thousands of people all in one place.

That is why small business owners need their support and information in different ways – and at different times! If you're running a small café or shop, you can't take a day off for training – that has to happen out of normal hours. The Information has to be freely available in small chunks and on a need to know basis. Small business owners don't really have the luxury of knowing loads of things that aren't relevant at this precise moment. This can lead to crisis management and it's much more difficult to plan and strategise in that environment. But many small businesses manage and flourish in that environment, so it can be done.

Therefore, the best approach to development and management of a small business is to create an overall plan, and head towards it. Then break that journey down into small manageable pieces of information, knowledge and experience and just get on with it one step at a time.

Small businesses will never have the organisational structures of a large business, but that can be turned into a positive. One wo/man entrepreneurs can decide and act all in a heartbeat – that generally isn't possible for larger organisations.

And of course, what lies at the centre of every small business is the one person whose business it is: who carries the passion, responsibility and drive to make it happen and to make it successful.

This book is intended to suit the business owner. Information is in bite-size chunks for you to access as and when necessary and is not intended to be read in one go. It also includes lots of tips and tales from existing business owners so that you can discover the peaks and troughs of their experiences. This book is intended to be an 'how-to' practical guide for anyone who wants to start, manage or sell a business and includes lots of necessary detail and definitions in some sections like marketing and tax - so don't expect many jokes there. There will be something useful here for you, whatever the stage of your journey.

'To be successful, you have to have your heart in your business, and your business in your heart'- **Thomas Watson Sr., chairman and CEO of International Business Machines**

What the heck: why are we doing this?

Before we leap in and start on the practical matters, it is worth a crucial reality check.

Why on earth do you want your own business? There are many initial possibilities:

- you have no other way to support yourself or your family
- you have been made redundant from your existing job and can't find any immediate replacement
- you are frustrated by the lack of opportunities and reward from your employment situation - in short; you feel you could do better
- you are frustrated by the inadequacies of your employment, your line managers and employment situation - again you feel you could do better
- you want more control of your circumstances, time and activity
- you have bigger horizons: you want to earn more, expand more, develop and grow
- you want more MONEY!

These are all fantastic reasons for an entrepreneurial start and the more frustrated, fed up and angry you are at your current situation, the more motivation you will have to make the leap.

However, there is a saying from a new business owner

that goes something like:

I gave up my job working eight hours a day for my idiot boss, to end up working 12 hours a day for an even bigger idiot in myself.

Ideally, you are neither an idiot nor do you want to work ridiculously long hours (unless you choose to of course) but are you prepared for the negatives that initially occur? It is unlikely that your financial flows will be even, consistent or large in the early days. You may have to sacrifice family, leisure and relaxation time for a huge input and effort to the business.

People will try to put you off and in my experience, our loved ones and friends do a better job of that than any enemy we fear. They will definitely tell you that you ARE that idiot, but they do it with the best intentions. They will be uncertain themselves and will be unsettled and potentially insecure by your entrepreneurial behaviour. This is particularly difficult if you have a family and children to support, as you do not want them to be, or feel vulnerable in any way.

Times can be hard and you will also be fearful from time to time. It is useful to prepare yourself for these setbacks and, for example, have a small financial buffer to keep yourself going for the first couple of months. It is also vital to get some support from say local business groups or more formal governmental type commerce organisations – and get as much help and support as you can. Any connection you can make should offer you some reassurance and courage, and these relationships may also turn into business connections longer term.

It is also vital to prepare yourself mentally. If you always wanted to have your own business but never have. What has stopped you in the past? What held you back before? What internal dialogue may you be running that tells you you're never going to do it? In my view, it is this personal fear that inhibits business success far more than any external economic or practical restriction.

In order to encourage you here, let me assure you that there has never been a better time in our society to take control and to own your own business. The world becomes an increasingly smaller place as every day passes and it is now completely possible for a one wo/man band to outbid, outmanoeuvre and outsell some of our business giants. In many instances, the customer cannot even tell who is at the other end of the sales chain and small businesses may be more flexible and reactive to a potential sale, particularly by the internet, than the larger organisations that are restricted by management structures and processes.

'A big business starts small'- **Richard Branson**

I have also noticed an increasing move towards

individuals wanting to take control of their own situation, finances and future wealth rather than leave that to the hands of some employer who frankly doesn't really care about you and your family. We have had so many scams, scandals and mis-selling from organisations that we assumed were doing the best for us that we have lost trust and confidence in their ability to protect and provide for us with a job. Most people feel more comfortable knowing their fate is in their own hands, particularly when we have so much evidence that our governments and our larger businesses aren't really doing a very good job these days.

We also know that the job for life is no longer really practical. We apparently change jobs somewhere between 10 and 15 times in a working life nowadays dependent on skill set, experience and personal circumstances. It is much easier to flex our working environment if we have our own business than it could ever be whilst working for somebody else who has their own rules, strategies and circumstances to worry about; in that situation, the employee just becomes faceless 'cannon fodder'.

At the end of the day, it's your life and your choice and I suggest you take some time now to think clearly about what you want to achieve from your own business and broadly where you think it could go. To help with that, what follows in the next section is a broad outline of a typical business growth pattern.

For me personally, my life has been more fulfilled, satisfied and successful in all measures since I have owned my own business. I was a traditional employee for many years working as a chartered accountant and in the financial services industry and although

that gave me fantastic experience, it never gave me any sense that my life had any business purpose or point to it. I never felt that I could influence anything or make a difference, whereas I see evidence every single day now that what my business does change lives for the better and there can be no better life mission for me than the achievement of that.

The overall business growth structure

The wealth motorway

If you have read any of my other books (if not start with Solving the Financial Success Puzzle) you will know that I believe in something called the wealth motorway. This means being invested in, or having access to, 3 main areas of financial and wealth accumulation, and they are:

- land and property,
- stocks, shares and trading of some kind, and finally
- owning a business.

There are separate books on both the property and

the trading lanes of the motorway (visit the shop at www.fjeldingfinancial.com to access the books) and in those books, you will see that I always create a pyramid structure for the development and growth of the investment in hand.

In summary, and for ease of reference, here are the property pyramid and the share trading and investing pyramids for you to see.

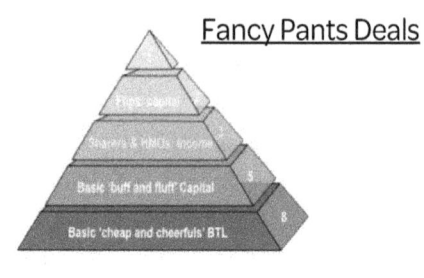

Fancy Pants Deals

- Flips: capital
- Shares & HMOs: income
- Basic 'buff and fluff' Capital
- Basic 'cheap and cheerfuls' BTL

Top Level Trading

Trading: For Example
Fancy Pants, Options, Dividend Chasing

Trading: Regular Action
Regular daily action: Shares, Indices or Currencies

Capital: Holding for Value
Long-term buy & hold strategy – fundamentals

Capital Investing
Simple capital strategies, year on year - SIPPs

Long-term Investing
Regular long term savings: Collective Compounding Investment Schemes, ISAs

The pyramid is a reliable and resilient structure and I use them to provide an overall strategy, to balance risk and reward, income and capital requirements and to provide coherence in my overall wealth accumulation. They also are complimentary and deliberately balance our time and money at different tiers of the pyramid such that we are not personally overexposed either financially or personally at any stage of our financial growth or development.

However, it is much more difficult to fit business as an activity into a standard formula or pyramid model, purely because each business tends to be quite different. We know that there are nearly 6 million SMEs (small to medium enterprises) in the UK alone, and that's a lot of different business approaches to consider.

The business also tends to be almost entirely an income-driven strategy – until the very end when, if it is sold, it provides a big capital gain (we hope!).

The life cycle of a business can be categorised into our standard Five Tier strategic structure as follows:

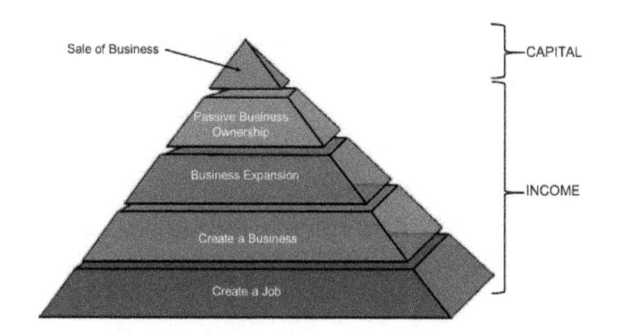

The bottom four tiers are income-generating entirely with the capital gain coming only at the very top or end of the business cycle with the sale of the business. Most business never gets to that top level for a variety of reasons, but most businesses would benefit strategically if they thought that it would!

Tier One: Creating a job

Many millions of new businesses are started every year and there is a significant majority of those started by a person who wants to create a job for themselves. Their intention is only ever to be a one wo/man band and if that works for them, that's fine, but I wouldn't really describe that as a business because what they are doing is swapping their time for money – I call it the 'stitch one, bill one' type of business where the person has to do one thing for someone else in return for one bill or invoice, and subsequent payment. There is no leverage there and if the business owner can't work, then there's no income.

That might sound risky but there is a certain amount of control and responsibility attached to it after all, nobody can ask you to do a role you don't want to do and nobody can make you redundant!

'Some people dream of success, while other people get up every morning and make it happen' - **Wayne Huizenga, prolific American business person, owner of Blockbuster Video & the Miami Dolphins**

In today's world, we know that a job for life is no longer possible and most people now have to cope with ups and downs, and periods of unemployment or changes in career path. Being employed isn't all that easy and so for some people the self-employed option is preferable.

However, self-employment like this is really akin to having a job and even worse, as soon as the business owner stops work then the business itself stops and it has no intrinsic value. There are no holidays, sick days, 'duvet' days or redundancy pay here.

Tier Two: Creating a business

The next step up is to take the 'stitch one, bill one' sole trader type of business and include someone else, as that then adds a different dimension. As soon as there is another person in the business, the level of responsibility goes up and the business suddenly becomes more than just a one wo/man band job creation scheme.

NB By another person in the business I mean an 'external' person who isn't your partner or relative helping you out. If however your partner is also your business partner then that sort of counts but there is a big difference when you suddenly have responsibility for feeding another family that isn't your own.

As soon as another person is involved, part of the business becomes passive. If, for example, you are a hairdresser and you take on another stylist who does their own customers but pays you a proportion of their earnings for the 'chair' and other overheads, that part of your income is now passive and will come in irrespective of whether you're styling hair or not.

Or if you're a consultant, or any service provider, a sink fixer or electrician, if you have an assistant who can work – even at a basic level – unaided, then you're on your way to creating a passive business that has value beyond you personally, as you now have something to sell: a set of customers and some method of getting some work done without you. At this stage, you can take a day off work and have fun or work on your success target – without any major damage being done to your income or finances.

However, at this level, you can't go far or take too much time off unless you build up your team of staff to be able to cope entirely without you. However, at this stage the business owner would probably still have responsibility for any customer 'schmoozing', and you must be very careful not to just drop your customer relationship management as most clients will still want to feel important and as if they have access to the boss.

Usually, at this level, the original business owner is still responsible for bringing in the work, even if it's completed in the main by other people.

At this stage, you could now sell the business for a fair value as you have a list of customers and product deliverers who could exist without you although, in these circumstances when businesses are sold, the original owner normally gets tied in by the new owners with a consultancy type of contract for a period of time, to make sure that the hand over goes smoothly, and that customers are not lost.

If you have sold or released, some capital with a sale you have also forfeited the right to the income generated by the business. And this is your choice and will depend on what money you need, when and why – but you will get a lot more capital, and a higher price, for your business if you take it up to the next level of expansion.

Tier Three: Expansion

The expansion means taking the business into a multi-dimensional level: so simple examples would be opening a second shop, employing a second team of service providers (not managed by you) or engaging sales through a different distribution channel. For instance, you may have only ever traded on the web and now you open a shop, or you may have only ever sold B2B (Business to Business) but now you create a retail – direct to the customer - option.

The aim is to make the business multi-faceted and to take the business one step further away from your personal management, and in order to do that, you have to use procedures and systems to provide the control of the business rather than personal instruction. Just imagine if McDonald's had to make every meal with a supervisor, rather than as it does, with a low-skilled worker working to a completely systemised process? Every meal would take an age and cost a fortune.

Furthermore, every meal would taste a little bit different and that variation is critical to a business and is very damaging. If a customer returns, what they want is what they expect and they want it exactly the same as the last time they bought your service or used it. Customers like certainty, even if that level of product or service isn't quite ideally what they want – if they know for certain exactly what they are going to get it leaves them 'satisfied' with what they get. If the level of delivery or product varies too much, the customer becomes unsettled and won't stay with you and repeat buy. As it's far cheaper to keep an existing customer than it is ever to get a new one – do whatever you can to hold on to the customers you have and ensure that if they want the exact same service again – they know where to get it and come to you.

The aim is to create a procedure so accurate and systemised that IT creates and controls your product or service rather than you, in a completely repeatable way constantly and consistently every time.

Tier Four: Passive Business models

Once you are at this level of systemisation you are almost ready to sell that business and Tier Four is about being able to sell that business and maximise your capital gain with a product or service that works on its own, and this requires taking the systemisation and procedures to a new level.

What you have to imagine is that your business is purely a set of instructions: procedures manuals, that are so accurate that any person could open the manual at page one and replicate the business. Everything would be in those manuals: timings, planning, phone numbers, contact details, shop opening times, customer discounts, supplier agreements, how to wrap a product, what codes to use for the till and the accounting system – EVERYTHING that your business does, in a step-by-step guide, with diagrams, and illustrations and examples of paperwork and even examples of the product itself if appropriate.

Then if you went under a bus today and 'left' the business, then another person could pick up the manuals and keep the business going exactly as it is. Those manuals are now the value in the business – not you!

And NOW it's completely saleable and NOW you have options to generate either income or capital and as much as you like because you could sell an income option with a franchise – and not only get a capital lump sum for selling the franchise (or the procedures manuals) but also probably get a regular income from the royalty or license from the franchisee for using 'your' information, copyright and contracts for instance. Some franchises also include regular marketing materials and web support for instance – and as long as you have built the system and the procedures manual for those things, you can command more capital and more income.

OR you could just sell the whole darn thing and get a higher price and a larger chunk of capital, but of course, you then forgo the regular income from the franchisees.

Your business – your wealth – your choice.

Tier Five: Exit and sell that business!

At Tier Five you are now working ON the business and not IN the business as your day-to-day activity is about leading the business strategically, its profile and position within the overall market it is in and expanding it. You will also spend your time looking for a completely different type of customer – and that's one that will buy the whole business or a chunk of it, or a license to trade it rather than that one customer you first wanted to buy just one product.

For you, as the business owner, you now need to learn a whole new set of marketing skills. The market is different; the customer is different and they are looking for completely different things. In all probability, you will need expert help and guidance here.

This is where you cash out on all your efforts and go on holiday! But in order to do that you need to start planning a long way out: potential business purchasers want to see steady long-term sales and profit trends rather than erratic peaks and troughs; they need to see stability and prudence – and the more you have of all those, the more your business is worth. These longer-term issues are not your priority in the early days but it is worth keeping the thought in the back of your mind from the outset – as somewhere along the line that may help you make a better decision.

Summary: Business sections

There are many ways to divide up a business and what it does, but for ease of reference this book is divided into four main sections:
- sales funnel
- the business processes and delivery
- reporting, and
- leadership.

The Sales Funnel

This area will cover everything you need to know to sell one product to one customer: and that's:
- profile and positioning of the business and the product
- marketing and lead generation
- sales and sales methodologies
- follow up care and database management
- the internet and virtual world, and other connected topics.

The Process

The process will cover everything to do with the formula of the product, and getting it from you to the customer plus a few tips on the office world, organisation structures and HR.

Reporting

Now reporting for me doesn't mean what it generally means to everyone else and although we do have to report to external bodies, my view is that those reports are purely a by-product of what we need for the more important information providing purposes for our business leadership and management. This management information is the overriding purpose of any records you keep and this will be covered in detail, but we will also cover:
- the legal setup, and business and internet names
- ongoing external secretarial duties
- relevant taxations
- compliance and regulatory requirements
- trade bodies and other organisations

Leadership

And this section is all about you, the business leader and what you're meant to be doing for the business and for yourself!

Leadership may seem to be an odd one to be included in a basic business book but actually as we will see this may be the most important thing for a business owner to address.

In most cases, the practical information is the easiest

section to grasp and the control of yourself and your emotions is the most difficult area.

We will cover both people and business leadership.

Each section will be subdivided further into these topic element areas that you can dip in and out of and everything a business owner does, whatever the size of the business, can be fitted into these categories. Everything is here to enable you to live a life of financial freedom, control, security and profit.

Strap yourself in and enjoy the ride!

THE SALES FUNNEL

Introduction

We need to start with sales as our primary objective. If we can't sell anything, then we have nothing but a curious hobby. When you watch business investment programmes such as Dragon's Den or Shark Tank, you will notice that the expert investors focus firstly on sales opportunities. They are always interested in whether any orders have already been obtained and by that they mean orders not obtained from friends and family. As soon as there is a contract for sale the value of the business immediately jumps up.

It is a common mistake for novice entrepreneurs to focus initially on the process or periphery items such as logistics and administration. In my opinion, this is a mistake. My guidance is that anyone who wishes to start an entrepreneurial journey starts first with trying to sell just one item of their product to an independent person, i.e., not a friend or family member. You don't need fancy paper or lighting in that instance to quickly evaluate whether you have a business idea that has some future.

What you are seeking for with this initial sale is the feedback that you are on the right path and all the logistics, admin, lighting and so on can quickly be put into place shortly after. There is no point in wasting any money on anything other than the basic product until you are sure that that is the product you need.

Sadly, too many people are in love with a crazy idea

they have had after a few beers or glasses of wine and at that stage, the product is a world-beater. In order to see your potential product without the 'beer goggles', you need to expose it to the outside world and discover if anyone else shares your enthusiasm.

However, once you have that feedback then we need to go full steam ahead on creating a sales funnel.

The sales funnel may be a fairly outdated term nowadays, but it's a good description of what we are attempting to achieve. Firstly, we need to engage with the outside world and drive people into our arena. This I refer to as the marketing process and would include PR, profile and external positioning in this section. What the marketing process does is make the outside world aware of who you are and broadly what you do and is the start of your potential customer list, or database. Therefore, we will also cover database management and capture here. Once we have that database, we need to sell to it.

This is where we convert the lead into cash going into business. This is our second section – the SALE!

Our final section in the sales funnel is the post-sale

and virtual world. We will include in this section everything to do with the Internet, the web, and any social media activities.

The three sections work together as a group. We attract leads; we sell - or attempt to sell - to those leads and if they don't initially buy; we need to find a way to take the lead back into the database for further marketing and customer care. You will soon realise that your leads are a valuable asset: you pay a lot of money and put in a lot of effort to gain those leads, so once you have them look after them carefully. Keep them warm, love them and contact them regularly.

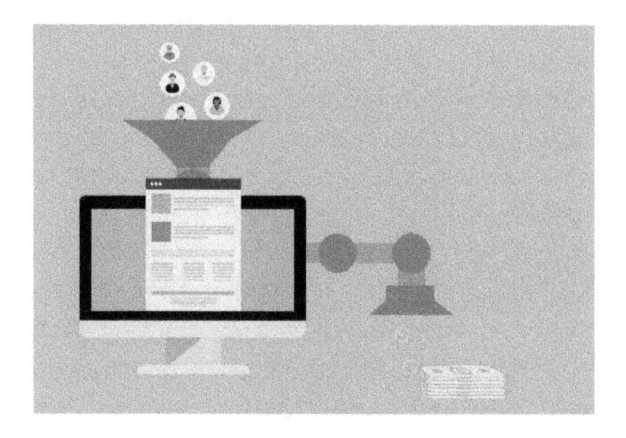

The Internet we will address as a separate topic altogether partly because it is such a large area these days not only covering the whole business in every area but also because it straddles our two areas of marketing and sales. We can use the virtual world across every area of the sales funnel from positioning, profile, PR, direct sales, repeat sales, and so on. We can also use the web across the globe and the Internet has provided a worldwide opportunity for any business owner.

A. Marketing

N.B. I suggest you dip in and dip out, on a need to know basis, in this section. It includes all a business owner needs to know but it can be heavy reading as a whole.

Marketing & Social Media: Before the sale

The vast majority of marketing takes place before the sale, although some also takes place after a successful sale – as well as after a sale approach has failed. In broad terms marketing is the way you let people know that you're in business and that you have a fantastic product or service to sell. Once you've had the idea and you've formed your business plan and you're on your way to creating your product, you now need to create a marketing plan. Fundamentally what's a business or a product if no-one knows about it?

This is where a solid marketing strategy comes in useful. At this stage, you need to be thinking about the image you want to put out there, your tone of voice, how you want to present yourself to your customer. There are some easy questions to answer that will help you work this out and we'll cover some fun exercises that will help you think differently and help bring your business brand to life. First, let's cover the basic topics and questions, to help get you in the mindset to start thinking about how you are going to develop your marketing.

'Content builds relationships. Relationships are built on trust. Trust drives revenue'- **Andrew Davis, Author &Keynote speaker, Monumental Shift**

So 'Marketing' what's it all about then?

Marketing is a bit of an enigma to most people, as it is very much a jack of all trades topic. Marketing generally connects all aspects of a business, the messaging and promotion of the product, being a brand guardian and making sure the look and feel of the business is consistent in attracting new customers. Marketing doesn't end there, the job of a marketer is also to nurture the customers acquired by making sure they stay loyal and if possible, buy additional products.

Why 'brand' is important

It's important for you to think about your brand as it needs to be personal to you and your business. It's the silver thread that will tie everything you do together and also what will make you stand out from everyone else in the market. Your brand is the 'outward' thing that, if you and your employees live it every day, will show your authenticity, build customer trust and capture the attention of prospective customers.

NB The term customer, audience and leads will be used interchangeably throughout.

PR – is that any different from marketing?

The answer is yes! Although the two work very well side by side the job of marketing and PR is slightly different. PR, or Public Relations managers, have the sole responsibility of getting the product/brand/company/YOU talked about across the town, whilst being responsible for managing your profile and reputation. PR companies have huge networks that they've nurtured over the years and it's through these networks that they can secure the interviews, spots on the radio and TV appearances.

Strategy – do I need one?

Like setting goals, a marketing strategy will help you visualise where you want to be in the next year, five years or even ten. It'll run in tandem with your business strategy and will keep you on the straight and narrow to achieving your vision for your business.

Eek! Sounds scary and like a lot of hard work. Depending on your situation you may be able to outsource this work to an agency, however, if you're just starting out the purse strings can be understandably tight, and that's why we've pulled together some top tips, ideas and a few diagrams to help get you started.

How do I start to create 'marketing'?

A good place to start is with your business strategy, the business objectives, any identified Key Performance Indicators - KPI's - and include any financial targets. Review all those to remind yourself of the ingredients that will help form the marketing steps you need to take to get to your end goal. This is also the place where you can dream your biggest dreams, write them down and let's see if we can make or at least tailor some of those to be a reality.

For reference, marketing will be broken into easy to digest sections:

a) Marketing – Research
   1. SWOT
   2. Audience Demographics and Profile
   3. The Competition

b) Marketing – Branding
   1. Values for the company
   2. Value to the customer
   3. TOV (Tone of Voice)
   4. Mission or Vision Statement

      5. Tagline
      6. Branding and Guidelines
      7. Website or your shop window

c) Marketing – Strategy
      1. Planning
      2. Implementing the Plan

And finally, all the other stuff such as...

- PR
- Radio
- Freebies and how giving a little earns a lot

There are also other critical topics such as the website, CRM (Customer Relationship Management) tools, digital and social media and we'll look at those after the Sales sections as part of our post sale marketing.

What is SWOT?

Start by with reviewing the business strategy, objectives, KPIs and goals and then take a piece of paper and divide it into four as you need to do a SWOT analysis of your business, it's position and that of your competitors. There are no 'right' or wrong answers but this is something that you can start with and look at from time to time and adjust with changing circumstances.

SWOT stands for Strengths, Weaknesses, Opportunities and Threats.

Consider each of these and write down anything or anyone that springs to mind.

Strengths	Weaknesses
Product test reviews came back 98% positive Customer love the design	*Start-up with not much finance behind the business*
Opportunities	Threats
Not many products like this on the market Market competition is low Chance to shine and find financial backing	*If successful could become a competitive market*

Although it could seem counterproductive looking at the negatives, it is a useful exercise to consider every aspect of what could go right and what could go wrong. The aim is to consider how to turn any weaknesses and threats into strengths and opportunities. It also helps you to position yourself and how you feel about your business.

Who is my customer or audience?

The SWOT helps to guide you to the position of your business and now we need to add an audience, and some customers who will buy our product. We can divide our customers into a primary and secondary audience with the primary audience being the 'lowest hanging fruit' i.e the people who are likely to easily bite and jump at your product. We then have our secondary audience, who are the customers that have longevity and although we may have to work a little harder to convert, it'll be worth it in the end as once they buy they'll tend to stick for a long time and repeat buy. Most businesses need both types of customers: some to buy quickly to get immediate cash in the door but who may not necessarily be long term loyal, and those who may take longer to make a buying decision, but once they're customers, they are loyal customers for life.

How can I find out more about my target audience?

There are plenty of resources out there that will tell you everything you need to know about your target audience such as facts and figures, buying habits, what they earn and even where they live. Useful resources are the ONS, Statista and Ofcom reports, where you can find the nitty-gritty numbers. From here you can start building the potential audience profile, and what the ideal customer looks like. For instance:

Age: 25-44
Gender: Male 50% / Female 50%
Demographic: ABC1 (C1, C2)
Average Income: £34,000
Location: London, Reading and Basingstoke

Now you've got a clearer idea of who you want to talk to, it's time to give them a little bit of personality and essentially make the customer jump off the page.

For this, you'll need to mix a little bit of research with imagination, and put yourself into your customers' shoes and understand more about them. Think about their interests and behaviours. Do they like to party on a Saturday night or do they stay at home? Are they an adventurous outdoorsy person or someone who likes to relax in a spa or stay at home? Each of these different behaviours and interest will impact you because some groups will never be interested in your product and some will. For those that will, consider how to attract them with your messaging and branding.

It is also worth considering what could drive your audience to buy your product or attend your event: why should they buy from you? How can you address their need state? Make a list of points. These could include: They need to get out of their current rut, they want to earn more money so they can go on luxurious holidays or they want to quit their job and be financially free! Then work out how can you, your brand and your company appeal to their need state?

The Competition

Undertaking an analysis of your competitors is a worthwhile task, after all, you don't want to create a logo and tagline that doesn't set you apart or find out that you've accidentally used theirs because you've subliminally absorbed their marketing!

Whilst undertaking your analysis look at the colours they use, what their message is, is their tone of voice corporate or friendly? Do they showcase their price points? Sign up to their newsletters to see what kind of information and resources they send out. Do they give away a freebie?

From this exercise, you'll gain a little more clarity on what you like and what you don't and more importantly align your values working out who you admire and who you don't want to be.

It will also give you some guidance on what 'works' in your particular industry or market place.

Taking all those discoveries, analyses, and customer and competitor awareness, now consider the branding!

Branding includes all the things that present our look and feel such as logos and website design, for example. Luckily there are plenty of people out there who can help for free or not much money at all so we don't have to be a branding expert ourselves here.

When you start out branding your business and product it's useful to think not just about how you're going to look but also how you will sound, so your tone of voice. You also want to consider your values, what do you want to portray to your customer and live and breathe internally as your brand can reflect those.

Values for your Company

You may have all the answers here but note down what you believe your business values to be and if you're a solopreneur what do those look like for you personally as the two, may go hand in hand.

To clarify your values list words that 'fit' your company, words that feel right, and will act as an indication of how you want your company, brand or yourself to be seen.

These could be:
Honest

Determined
Hard-working
Funny
Informative

Once you find a list that is right for you and really resonates what you want it's time to print it, put it front and centre and make sure that anything you do from calls to press ads radiates those values.

And, if you're truly aligned with your values, this will eventually become another powerful instrument in your marketing tool kit. Your customer will recognise it, they will expect and appreciate it and more importantly, if they believe in your values too, they will be a loyal customer.

If you'd like to take it a step further, put yourself in your customers' shoes and tweak your list so it works externally too. For example:

Honest becomes trustworthy
Determined becomes dedicated
Hard-working becomes customer first
Funny becomes uplifting
Informative becomes reliable

Have a play and see what fits. Once you have your list, it'll be a lot easier to stay on track with your marketing efforts.

Value to your customer

It's time now to think about what value or benefit your product has or can offer to potential customers. This can be done by asking a few simple questions, looking at the benefits to your core market and the images and ideas that you want to project.

The benefits:
The Customer gets... Include the value of owning the product, how will it enhance that customer's life?
The Customer can... By purchasing your product how will it change your customer's life?

Images/ Ideas:
The Audience sees... Think about the first thing the customer will see, what will your visuals and messaging portray to the customer.
The Audience thinks... What do you want your customer to take away from the first encounter with your business?
The Audience believes... If the customer buys into your product, what will your customer believe will happen if they purchase?
These can seem like big questions, so I'll use Fielding Financial Property Investing as an example:
The Audience sees... A professional training company.
The Audience thinks... They are getting the best education and opportunities.
The Audience believes... They will become a valued and successful family member.

It's worth noting at this point that it's not all going to be roses, but what we can do is think ahead and more specifically identify some of the concerns early on.
So, we've thought about why the customer will fall in love with your product and why they see value in making a purchase, but what about those who have concerns?

You've most likely come across the age-old marketing adage, the Rule of 7. This idea is that a customer will need to 'hear' your message 7 times before they take action or buy your product. So, if they buy after one message or touch point that's a win, however, don't get disheartened if your customer takes a little longer to 'bite'.

What we can do is an exercise to pre-empt those who take a little longer or have 'concerns". Another quick exercise, put yourself in your customers' shoes. What can they see that is a possible turn off? Is it the price? Is it fear or scepticism that what you're selling might not work? Now just like the SWOT exercise, take these concerns and turn them on their head, use these points in your marketing; counter act cost concerns by showing that you are either the cheapest or if your product is more expensive than others on the market, tell the customer why it is and why it is worth it. Fear and scepticism, for example, often come hand-in-hand and can be difficult to overcome, but that doesn't mean they can't be.

Recognise that your customers are only human, they make decisions emotionally, just as much as they do rationally. What can you do to get them on side? Can you use testimonials either video or written, or make an extra call to dispel a customer (or leads) fear? The answer will be different for every business, but remember concerns can be flipped on their head and turned into a strength and/or opportunity.

Tone of Voice (TOV)

Finding your tone of voice is essential to keep your

marketing on track, and a consistent tone of voice is one of the things that can act as a constant thread and help a customer know when it's your business 'speaking' to them.

The tone of voice (TOV) should be personal to you and your business, there is no point in pretending to sound or be something you aren't as eventually you'll slip, and it'll be confusing for the customer.

Your TOV should also align with your values, if you've said light-hearted or funny as a value then that should come across in your communications, if you've said professional and business-like that should also come across. Selecting a TOV for your business should come naturally and to that end sound natural too. If we look at Nike as an example, their famous tagline is 'Just Do It' its straight to the point and reflects Nike's motivational stance and values. It also embraces their mission and every business needs to have, and be proud of, their mission or vision and be able to state it simply and in 'taglines'.

Mission or Vision Statement Vs. Tagline

A Mission or Vision Statement is something that you can use internally or externally, it reflects the ultimate direction of the business and identifies what the business is about. The mission statement may be tweaked as the business gains clarity but this ultimate purpose will run throughout all you do in the business. It will also direct business goals and objectives that you set for the years to come.

If the mission is crystal clear it will also help build associations and recognisability of your company and business.

Your mission or vision statement doesn't have to be paragraphs long; a couple of lines should do the trick. For Fielding Financial, the ultimate mission is 'to light the spark of financial possibility for as many people as we can get to' and that remains constant but 'sub missions' or parts of that mission can be emphasised or marketed externally and internally each year. For 2018 it was to 'light 1 Million sparks', for 2019 it was slightly longer and more celebratory 'Happy 10th Anniversary, 10 years of togetherness, 10 years of happiness, 10 years of making dreams come true, 10 years of trust, 10 beautiful years'.

You need to get clear on the business mission or purpose so think about what you want this to achieve, and where do you want to be in 1, 5, 20 years' time? It can be as big or small as you want, but it's important to get it on paper so it's tangible and so it is shareable with your colleagues and staff.

Start by brainstorming or writing some ideas:

Our mission is to...

.... and let the pen flow. See what emerges . Ideally make it short and clear and uncomplicated. The best mission statements are short, sweet and easy to remember. It'll take a few goes and can be a challenge to craft at first, but keep going it'll fall into place.

Now we've covered our mission or vision statement it's time to think about your tagline or slogan. A tagline is a little different, it's purely external or customer-facing. It is the line that will remain with your business for a long time and shouldn't be changed frequently as it's a 'tool' that will help build your business and recognisability. It's shorter or to the point and designed to be memorable, remember Nikes 'Just Do It' tagline?

Presenting Your Marketing Findings

You can document your marketing findings in a variety of ways, as long as it makes sense to you, that's all that counts. I would recommend using the headings so far as a guide. It's also useful to create a tailored version for yourself and any reader and a quick snapshot of your marketing work thus far will act as a useful reminder to yourself or conversation starter.

This template is quick and easy to fill in and highlight the essential information. Go back over your notes and marketing findings and insert the top-line information.

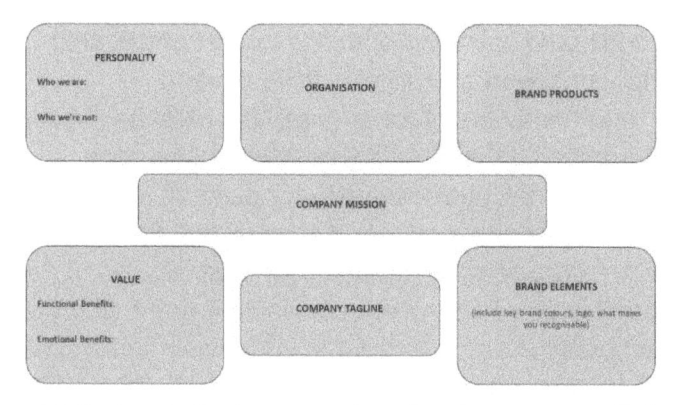

PERSONALITY	ORGANISATION	BRAND PRODUCTS
Who we are:		
Who we're not:		

COMPANY MISSION

VALUE	COMPANY TAGLINE	BRAND ELEMENTS
Functional Benefits:		(include key brand colours, logo, what makes you recogniseable)
Emotional Benefits:		

Well done! You've completed a huge part of the background work that goes into forming your business's marketing. Next, we will take all that information and translate it into a brand – and by brand, we mean the visual stuff that will bring your business to life and give your product a platform and make it stand out.

Are you creative? Branding Your Business

Designing a brand without being creative yourself can be difficult, but luckily there are plenty of people out there who can help bring your vision to life.

Websites such as www.upwork.com and www.bark.com have a host of freelancers ready to take on creative projects for a much smaller rate than say a creative marketing agency. If you need logo websites such as www.99designs and www.fiverr.com can help.

To brief any external worker, simply pull together all the information you have gathered so far, the snapshot on the previous pages and begin to write a short brief for what you want. Remember to be clear on who you are and what you want to convey. If you can pull together a mood board or images of things you've spotted that you think could work and aligns with your brand.

Another useful tool to use to share background information is the 'if my business was a...' exercise.

The 'if my business was a...' exercise is all about using daily objects or people to draw out different ways of thinking creatively about your business. So, if your business was a car, which car would it be? A trusty VW Golf, with traits such as reliable, well-known and practical OR is your business more like a Lamborghini, flash, expensive and fun to drive?

Or, if your business was a celebrity who would it be? Fiona Bruce with traits such as the approachable, voice of authority and aspirational OR is your business more like Rylan Clarke, fun, upbeat and savvy?

Use the template below to work out visually what/ who your business is most alike, or you want it to be like. Think about the traits of those items, people or animals.

CAR	PERSON/ CELEBRITY	ANIMAL
Car Brand/ Name Traits	Celebrity Name Traits	Animal Name Traits
PIECE OF FURNITURE	SPOKESPERSON	DRINK
Item of Furniture Name Traits	Spokesperson Name Traits	Drink Name Traits

Here are Fielding Financials so you can see it in action:

CAR	PERSON/ CELEBRITY	ANIMAL
VW Golf Reliable, trusted, well-known, owners do their research, practical yet fun	**Fiona Bruce** Approachable, voice of authority, trusted and aspirational.	**Eagle** Fearless, powerful vision, nurturing, tenacious and higher flyers.
PIECE OF FURNITURE	SPOKESPERSON	DRINK
Dining Room Table Circular, equal, multi-purpose	**Gill Fielding** Respected, popular, informative Inspirational	**Coffee** Energetic, warm, strong, straight forward, does as it says on the tin.

Another useful thing to recognise is that people can be logical or creative in their method of thinking, so in marketing terms make sure you present your brand in a way that suits the individual you are talking to or working with and provide both words and images.

Brand Guidelines

'Your brand is what people say about you when you're not in the room'- **Jeff Bezos, Founder & CEO Amazon**

Once you're clear about your logo, brand colours and those attributes that will help your business stand out, you'll need to create some brand guidelines.

Brand guidelines are essential for any business no matter how big or small. It's all about keeping your business look and feel consistent and recognisable. If you stick to the rules set out in the brand guidelines, you'll easily be able to build awareness and become the brand that sticks in an individual's mind (especially useful when it comes to the marketing 'Rule of 7').

Writing brand guidelines is another exercise in

collating the surrounding information into an easy to digest document. Hopefully, your designer will have provided some information so you can easily cut and paste that into your document.

Some of the things worth including are:

Your logo rules, what can it sit next to, light or dark colours? Can you separate the elements if it's a mix of words and image?
Your brand colours, what are the hero/main colours? What do these work well with? Include the hex, RGB and CYMK numbers for ease.
Your fonts, what should you use on your emails, website, leaflets and press ads?
Do you have any rules on designs for press ads, banners, video content?

From colours and fonts to how your business cards and letterheads look should be included in this document. Again, with a document like this to hand it would be difficult to stray, and it ensures that your brand remains holistic across your business efforts.

Get Yourself A Shop Window

Nowadays a website is an essential marketing and sales tool for your business and product. It is your digital shop window and most likely the first place potential customers are going to look for you, your business and products. We are in a digital age where everything is at the tip of your fingers, so building an online presence is essential if you are to succeed.

Depending on your budget, there are various ways you can go about creating your website. If you don't have a lot to spend, there are free platforms such as www.wix.com and www.squarespace.com which includes easy to populate templates and user guides to get you started. You can also add shop functionalities and connect them to your CRM – Customer Relationship Management – tool, but more on that later.

If you have a small to medium size budget, you can approach freelance website designers through the platforms mentioned earlier www.upwork.com and www.Bark.com, simply upload your brief, have conversations and select the person who best understands and resonates with your business, and has the experience.

Now, if you have a larger budget, you can always engage with a digital agency and brief the project to them. This will tend to cost around £4K upwards, but it will be worth it.

Each of these options will get you started and as your business grows, so will your revenue and therefore budget to do more with your website. The most important thing is to ensure that your user experience (UX) is the smoothest it can be. There is nothing worse than getting to a website and not being able to navigate around or purchase the item you've been geared up to buy!

*When talking to designers you may be asked what's more important UX or UI, ideally, you have both. UX stands for User Experience and UI stands for User Interface, which means the design features.

Creating and Growing a Database

Your database is and will be your most valuable asset, so it's important to look after and nurture it from the start.

There are a variety of CRM (Customer Relationship Management) systems out there with varying price points and functionality. To find the system that best suits your business I'd recommend doing your research, talking to the platform providers and seeing a demo. As mentioned there are plenty out there, but to name a few, Fielding Financial, for example, use www.InfusionSoft.com by Keap, other companies swear by www.Kartra.com, and then there are also free options designed to get you started such as www.MailChimp.com and www.Hubspot.com. Depending on your business needs the last two could very well be just what you need in the early stages of launching your business and marketing.

A CRM system will help you manage and grow your business far more effectively than if you were to use a spread sheet! CRM systems allow you, as a business owner, to manage your relationships with your customers and/or other businesses, it holds their data and information (including their purchase history and behaviours) and allows you to interact with them on a personal level. You can see and monitor a customer's actions, what they've bought: if they have opened one email type over another, and you can tailor your marketing efforts to suit that individual and ultimately drive more sales.

You can also create lists and segment your audience by tracking their actions, for example, if 50% click a link to a deal and 50% don't then you can email the 50% who did with a follow-up email and try to entice them further.

Your database is your most valuable asset as the chances are you've already paid for the people on it to become a lead or customer through your marketing efforts and through your CRM system you will be able to nudge them closer to purchase or introduce them to new products and increase your sales.

NB: Please note the GDPR guidance regarding the storage of personal data.

But how do I get people into my database?

There are a few ways you can do this. A successful marketing effort, which we'll cover shortly, will lead to one of two places, a booking or purchase via a phone call or via your website. You can use the booking or purchase information to update the CRM system manually for any new customers. For anyone who comes through your website, your CRM can be integrated to your business systems or website so the customers information moves across automatically, so you don't have to do anything.

You can also add people to your database before they have purchased anything and you can build up your contacts, for instance, through a free newsletter sign up form or by offering a free informative download in exchange for a customer's details. You can encourage customers to give you their details by offering a free webinar or offer too.

At every stage add information and contact details to your database to create a valuable business asset that you can nurture and grow – and even sell to others if that's appropriate.

And once they are in my database?

Now, it's time to nurture! Each of the CRM systems mentioned above provides templates and easy to use guides on how to build what we call 'nurture' campaigns. These campaigns will be the tools that will manage the customer journey and help them flow towards a purchase.

An example of a nurture campaign could include the following emails:

A thank you for signing up email
Learn more about our business
Have you seen what we have to offer?
Special discount for our database only

A further benefit to using a CRM system is they will not only have campaign templates but also email templates so all the hard work has been done for you. Don't forget to include a mixture of content too from images to video, as a variety will keep your customer intrigued.

It's also worth noting how often you are contacting your database. We want to keep them interested but not push them to unsubscribe, so put yourself in your customers' shoes and ask how often do you want to hear from a company? And plan around that number.

As a marketer, your goal is to lead your customer to a sale. So, use your CRM system to hold your customer's hand, grow your relationship and entice them, send them special offers now and again and lead them until they've reached your goal.

Building Your Marketing Strategy

Firstly you need to consider how much money you have available, and in the main you need more! You should have a clear idea of your budget and how much you can spend on marketing from your initial business plans. However, it's helpful to start without the constraints of a financial budget and embark on some big picture thinking.

The idea is to think BIG and think impossible - get those, what may initially seem crazy, ideas on paper, don't worry about the budget or how difficult it will be to 'do' it. This is a chance to dream about where you want to see your business or product marketing – on the side of a plane, a Times Square billboard, and so on.

This exercise is a great planning tool and really gets you thinking outside the box, helping you to realise just how big your business and marketing could go. All these ideas can be made into goals and the 'wouldn't it be cool if...' moments set as milestones for the future.

For now, you're starting up so having your logo on a billboard without the big bucks is a little way off.

So take those ideas and apply them to your reality now and think about how you could get to the big picture with smaller steps – and smaller budgets – now.

Where do Marketers market?

There are several areas worth considering for marketing your business and your marketing efforts will fall into these categories or platforms:

Press
Radio

Television
Flyers and Letter Box Drops
Digital
Social Media
Email
PR
Networking

And of course, all these areas and efforts will help to divert traffic, customers (or business leads) to your website, product and business. Think about how each of these areas can help you by asking two questions:

1. What is the objective of using the platform?
2. How can I use it to achieve my goal?

'The best marketing doesn't feel like marketing.' - **Tom Fishburne, Founder & CEO Marketoonist**

Once you've answered these two questions, you're ready to start putting some plans into place.

First, let's cover each of the listed platforms above and how it can help you to market your business to the right people.

Traditional Media Vs Digital Marketing

Within the marketing sphere, you'll hear about two types, Traditional Media and Digital Marketing. Most businesses use both to get their message heard and product 'out there' and there's also not a one-shoe-fits-all approach. Go back to your market research and look at your target demographic and think about where your customer will 'be', this will give you a good indication of where to start marketing first.

What's the difference between Traditional Media and Digital Marketing? Traditional Media counts as Television, Radio, Press, Billboards and Flyers whereas Digital Marketing includes Video, SEO, Social Media, Display, Blogs and Email. Traditional Media allows you to reach the masses and increase your brand awareness exponentially whereas Digital Marketing can offer the same in terms of reach and awareness plus you also can be a lot more targeted and specific whilst reaching exactly who your pre-defined audience is. This also means that you can ensure a better cost per lead (CPL) and by this, I mean you pay less for introducing and initiating a customer to your business.

Let's look at each of these areas to decide what's the best fit for marketing your business and product.

'Digital marketing is not an art of selling a product. It is an art of making people buy the product that you sell.' - **Hecate Strategy**

Traditional Media in a nutshell...

Press:

Press is a great place to be spotted by hundreds of thousands of people, depending on the circulation of paper you opt for. It provides your business and product with a short exposure to a primed and already engaged audience. There's plenty of opportunity here, where you can book anything from a small box or strip to a full-page ad.

You can be as creative as you like with your advertisement or even create something in the style of an advertorial where there is more copy and it looks like an article. You can choose where you'd like to be placed, front, back or even take over the whole of the outside cover! Some insider advice; always opt for the right-hand side as this has a much higher chance of being read.

You may have spotted that specific days feature specific content, if this is the case as with Fielding Financial, opt for the property day if you're advertising property – your audience will already be in the right mind-set.

Radio:

Radio advertising is another form of traditional media, it's also 'portable'. By portable, I mean that you can reach an audience easily when they are out and about, whether walking, running or driving. Good radio advertising must be memorable so keep it short and to the point with strong creativity. Also remember to include your key message at the beginning and the end as this is will reinforce the piece of information you want to be remembered the most.

Radio advertising is relatively low cost compared to other traditional media and there are companies out there who will help you run traditional campaigns as well as more current ones like competitions. Competitions are a good way to accumulate leads into your database. When you're booking your radio campaign, opt for drive time as this is when most people will be commuting and a high as the possible frequency to successfully reach your audience.

Television:

Now, television is the most expensive form of media, and like press, there are a few large companies who control the media buying but there are also agencies who can secure you a discount selling the spots that have been released by the broadcasters. Television advertising has the greatest costs by far, and this includes creating your advert fit for television.

Like press and radio, you can be selective on where and when you want your advert to appear, however the more prime-time you go, or the more popular the programme, the more expensive it is.

When it comes to creating your advertising remember your audience and who you want to reach as television covers a broad spectrum and you need to be advertising at the right time, alongside the right programmes for your potential audience. The ad-breaks are typically when a viewer goes to pop the kettle on so be creative and make sure you catch their attention early. You also only have either 20 – 40 seconds to get your message across. Sounds intimidating, but if it's done right your brand awareness will sky rocket!

With the growth in Video on Demand (VOD) traditional and digital have crossed over. So, if television is perfect for your marketing strategy then explore the online option too. Be selective about the programming you want to feature around and consider sponsorship; broadcasting houses have departments that are dedicated to building these relationships.

Flyers and Letter Box Drops:

A low-cost form of traditional media is the flyer or letterbox drop. Design an advert to suit your needs and simply print 100 or 1,000 and deliver them to letter boxes. It's a manual job but is a great way to get out into the community you're trying to reach and make personal connections. Make sure your message is clear and that your advertisement includes how to either contact or find you. You may also want to consider a discount and physical coupon depending on the nature of your business – this will help reinforce the connection with your customer.

What about Digital Marketing?

Within this section, we'll cover each of the touch points within the digital world and how you'll be able to see how a combination of each can benefit the marketing of your business.

We will also be talking about 'rankings', the idea with digital marketing is to make sure you're seen and that you rank highly on the search engines i.e. Google or Bing. The higher you rank the more likely your website or social pages will appear on the first page when you search for either your business or the key terms that relate to your business.

Video:

Like television, video is a powerful way to creatively market your business, brand and product. There are plenty of ways you can share your content too, the most popular being www.YouTube.com and www.Vimeo.com.

The goal is to create video content engaging enough that the viewer will stop, watch and buy. Or another best-case scenario is that the viewer will share your video, and if shared enough times this will create a 'viral' effect. Using platforms like YouTube and Vimeo don't cost you a penny either but it does mean that you need to rely on people finding your channel or content organically. If you have a budget, you can place this behind promoting your video content and this means you'll be able to effectively place yourself in front of your target audience for a relatively low cost.

Video is something that can also be recycled across all your marketing platforms, from your website to social media.

SEO (Search Engine Optimisation):

SEO is a form of marketing designed to drive traffic or customers to your website, whether this is simply a couple of pages with a shop or a website with a fully functioning members area. SEO searches for key words, terms or phrases so make sure your website has each of the key terms you want to be recognised built-in behind the scenes of your website – this can include keywords, links and metadata. To make sure this is operating as it should you can;

Make sure you include keywords within any copy and ensure all the fields are filled out. Within WordPress, for example, there is a traffic light system which gives you handy tips for improvement.

When your website is being built, provide your website developer with a list of key terms you want to be known for and ask for this to be built into the copy and backend of the website.

Then hire a digital agency: most will run an audit to see how your website is performing with searches and then make recommendations for improvement. Some will do this for free but others will ask for a fee and then recommend a monthly package which will ensure you always rank top in your business and product field.

SEM (Search Engine Marketing)

This area of digital marketing requires a certain skill set, which you can teach yourself but if you have the budget, I'd recommend investing in a digital agency who can do this for you.

SEM includes the promotion of your business and/or product using search engines, such as Google and Bing. You can sign up to Google Ads and Microsoft Advertising (formerly Bing) which are management platforms and through here you can set up your marketing campaigns, allocate budget and upload your display banners (creative advertising assets and images). The great thing about this is that anyone who clicks on the banner will be taken directly to your website, which you'll be able to track.

The advantage of this kind of marketing is you can be highly specific in your targeting, from age, sex, location and even interests. You can also set up multiple campaigns so your messaging can be even more precise and therefore effective. Within these platforms, you are easily able to see how successful a campaign is and tweak accordingly to maximise campaigns that are working and for example, minimise budgets on those that aren't.

Display or Banners:

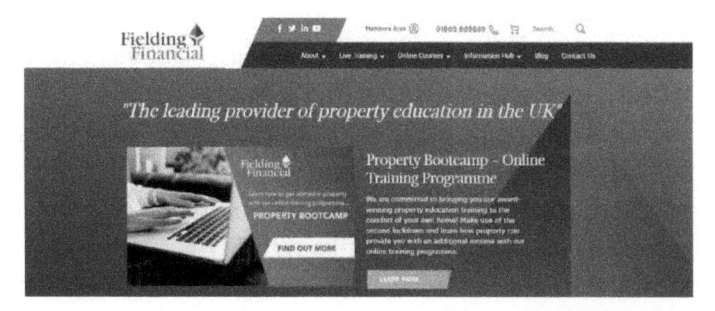

We've briefly mentioned display within the SEM section. The words display and banners are interchangeable, and not only used for advertising across the search engines but also you can use your banners to advertise on other people's websites or blogs. Depending on the size of the business where you want to advertise your product there will be a fee, and this can be calculated in two ways – either PPC/ CPC or pay/cost per click – meaning you only pay if someone clicks or there will be a pre-arranged flat fee so even if no- one clicks the person who will 'host' your ads will get paid regardless.

In general, display is a low-cost way of advertising and if you've done your research and the blog or page your advertising is placed on is an ideal fit you should see leads coming through to your website and awareness of your brand increased.

Blogs:

Blogging and blogging for others is another nifty tool that can be used to not only improve your ranking but also put you in the limelight as an expert in the field. Having a blog on your website and regularly adding engaging posts (with a few keywords thrown in of course) will help to improve your rank on searches, and also will help the buyer learn a little more about you and what you have to offer.

The more personable and approachable a brand is with a great story; the more your customers will trust you and hero your company to their friends (word-of-mouth is another great and free marketing tool).

You can also offer to write for other blogs, suggest doing an interview and offer to reciprocate. This way you can gain access to their audience.

Email Marketing:

Once you have built up your database and are attracting leads/customers to your website, you now need to nurture them . This group of people are already interested in what you have to offer because they've given you their details, or signed up to a newsletter and you now have their name and email address. Email marketing is the cheapest form of marketing if you are doing it to your own database and you can connect with these people and tell them about what's new in the business or if there are any product developments or offers. Your task is to engage with them and nuture them along the path to a product purchase. Make sure that your content is useful and compelling too as your contact always has the option to unsubscribe.

Other ways you can email market are through doing email-swaps or paid emails. Email-swaps are another great way to access someone else's ready-built database, just make sure you are of equal size as the swap must be a good 'deal' for both of you. Paid emails can be organised through agencies and your campaign manager will send your email to a specific email list of typically several thousand people who have shown interest in a product area. If they take action and click they will then enter your 'realm' and you will be able to market to them freely along with the rest of your database.

Social Media:

Now social media is another free tool that you can use to grow awareness of your brand. There are four main channels you should be on as a business, this includes Facebook, LinkedIn, Twitter and Instagram. Here you can build a following and relationship with your audience. This is a place where your brand personality can shine, and you can give your customers the inside track and daily goings- on. You can also use a mixture of content from video and images to long-form content which is essentially like a mini-article. It's important to engage with your audience too if they leave a comment or ask a question as this again helps show that you are an approachable contact on hand to help, which will help build trust and eventually lead to a conversion/ sale.

'Social media was designed to SHARE what you're doing and who you are, not BE what you're doing and be who you are'- **Richie Norton, Author**

Social Media Marketing:

This is where you take your social media to the next level and like search engine marketing you can be specific in your targeting and budgets. You can tailor it to an exact audience or simply 'boost' it to the masses. Social media marketing is the ideal companion to your organic social media activity, and both will enhance your presence in the digital world. As with all marketing messaging and creative, be clear on your key message and let the customer know exactly what they must do to buy into your product.

There's a handy guide on how to set up and get going with your social media and social media marketing after the sales section. Follow the step by step guide to get you started!

'Don't use social media to impress people; use it to impact people.' - **Dave Willis, write & pastor**

And what about PR?

As mentioned earlier, PR is all about managing and building your reputation as an individual and business and is best done via connections and relationships. PR managers work hard to build their networks and typically have nurtured all their relationships for years. They work in terms of earned media – this means they've not paid for it, but the media owner trusts them and their recommendations enough to promote their suggestions. You can also start to build your own relationships by reaching out to local media, bloggers and anyone else you think could help. The second option is to hire a PR manager or agency. You can do this for a single campaign or product or, if budget **allows, have them on a retainer**.

A good place to start before you embark on either route is to create yourself a press release. This should be one side of A4, include 3 or four paragraphs about yourself and product along with a few quotes and an image. It's a snapshot of what you have to offer and a conversation starter, attach to your introductory emails and go from there.

Networking

Networking is the perfect way to meet new people, whether they are potential customers or simply a supporter of your business.

Networking meetings happen nationwide on a variety of topics and you can easily search for ones near you using platforms such as www.Eventbrite.com or www.MeetUp.com. If you can't find anything of interest, set up your own! Again, it's easy using the above platforms.

Remember to pack your business cards and practice your elevator pitch in the mirror before you leave!

Next Steps

Now you have an overview of all the different places you can market it's time to get planning!

Go back and pick up your list of big ideas and ask yourself, what idea fits with which platform? Which ideas can be tweaked and changed to be possible now and in the next year? And finally, what can I develop now or what will take a few additional steps to build to?

It's important not to forget the excitement of the BIG ideas.

To begin your planning let's break it down into stages:

1. Select the marketing platforms that resonate most with your business and product.
2. For each platform write what the objective is and how you will achieve the objective i.e., what actions will you take?
3. Prioritise what will be actioned first, set a deadline and some goals or KPI's (key performance indicators) to keep yourself accountable and on track.
4. Carve out some time to get started!

Implementing Your Marketing Strategy

Now you have your marketing action plan in place, it's time to start implementing it, drive traffic and garner those leads that will essentially earn your money and keep your business going.

The most important thing is to keep going, start-up conversations in person or over email and follow up. If at a networking meeting someone shows interest swap business cards and reach out after. In the early days you are going to be your number one fan, so stay passionate and others will be passionate about your brand and business.

Reach out to as many people as you can, put in the effort and personalise your emails. Editors, publishers, radio producers get plenty of requests so think about how you can stand out and show yourself as a company worth listening to.

Be charming and see what you can get for free, whether that's a free press advert in your local paper or the opportunity to be interviewed or write an article. Don't say no – it's publicity and a chance for you to shout about the benefits of knowing about your business and buying the product or service.

Consider if you need help. You're starting a business after all and can't do everything! You can find freelance social media and copywriters on www.Bark.com and www.Upwork.com who for a small fee will write your blogs and newsletters and manage your social accounts from as little as 30 mins to a couple of hours a day.

Now, if you've got the budget, no problem! Once you have your creative assets ready, whether that's a press ad, copy driven advertorial or a set of display banners, you're ready to start contacting publishers, producers for the exact advertising spots you want and to start marketing online.

Whichever camp you fall into there's plenty of space out there to market and promote your product, so be savvy and keep schmoozing.

'Marketing is really just about sharing your passion.'-
Michael Hyatt, NY Times Best Selling Author

Anon; story

Having experienced big and unsettling changes in my life I decided to sign up for a free two hour Fielding Financial property seminar...this inspired me on a way forward and I signed up for the three days and then the whole package, which I am working my way along at my own (slow but steady) pace!

I am working from home with my very new company by myself and therefore.......

The top thing that has worked for me is the Networking and sharing of knowledge and ideas with other folks, at times of low motivation or when I have questions there is somewhere to go to seek help and encouragement.

The training has been first class and is always delivered in an upbeat, uplifting and informative way, with plenty of professional back-ups available.

The contacts made through Ptah meetings and a WIN support group in the Southwest have provided me with business partnering opportunities as I start my own journey into Property investing. I have met people from many different backgrounds who have opened my eyes to property possibilities, and we all share the same goal! Even though we are all going about it in a whole variety of different ways!

Confidence with myself has been a big issue and the personal quote I now live by, from Gills very mouth.... "Only do what only you can do" has been the most repeated phrase that I have used to reassure myself to get help when I need it and to tap into other people's expertise as I learn.... And that's ok to do and the best use of my time and is steering my course!

NETWORKING IS KEY!!!

B. Sales

Sales are one of those love 'em or hate 'em topics. Many people live in complete fear of just the thought of having to sell something to somebody else, whilst others can't wait to sell 24/7.

But if you can't convert a lead into a sale in some way or another you have no business, so if you're one of those hate 'em type of people then you need to find a way of getting to grips with it or delegating the process to somebody else.

Let's start with some principles that might get you thinking more positively.

There is an old adage that says that:

"sales are purely a transfer of enthusiasm about the product from one person to another".

And of course, what the initial business owner tends to have more than anyone else is enthusiasm for their product or service and so there is no sale as strong as the one that comes from the business owner. They generally believe in the product to their very core and also believe that everybody will love it as much as they do. And if you, as the initial business owner, don't believe in your product or service then the business will be much harder to run and will struggle to be successful.

Sales principles

1. Cheap products should be quick to sell and have a very low customer acquisition cost** associated with them.
2. Conversely, expensive products will take a very long time to complete the sales process and will have a high customer acquisition cost.
3. The higher the price of your product the longer you need to take to sell to the customer and the more likely that you will need to spend a significant time face-to-face with your potential purchaser.
4. The price of your product becomes less sensitive the more expensive it is. You see adverts every day on the TV where supermarkets are comparing the price of bread, for instance. It is clearly important when you are spending the small amount to get the price right and most supermarkets nowadays provide some cashback benefit to their shoppers based on these basic prices alone. A few pence or cents at this level represents a significant percentage of the overall price and consequently is regarded as being very price sensitive.

At the top end, however, price sensitivity tends to diminish. If you're buying a Rolls-Royce car you are hardly going to quibble over pence, cents or even a few thousand pounds, euros or dollars. At this level, the customer experience is much more important and people with this amount of money to spend certainly won't worry about the price. This is clearly a product that is not price sensitive.

However, there are exceptions to this rule and your product might be one. I always suggest every business does some price sensitivity checks at some stage, and moves the price up or down in a controlled and monitored way to see what impact that has on sales volumes.

Curiously you may find that putting the price up also increases the sales volume: customers aren't always logical and you need to perform these tests to see how they behave in certain situations.

5. You do need to get the price right. Cheaper products will tend to have a very low-profit margin consequently the highest volume of sales is needed to cover overheads and business running costs. A more expensive product tends to have a higher profit margin so you only need to sell one or two in order to provide the cash to run the business.

6. Price is not the only issue here and what the customer needs to perceive is that the price and the product match the value of what they are getting. In many cases, it is the value that the customer perceives that the product or service provides that makes the price acceptable. Therefore, you need to make sure that in your product descriptions and definitions that the value is clearly demonstrated and that holds true for any price product.

And finally,

7. The customer is on your side! Most people want 'stuff'. It gives them a sense of worth and validity and in many cases, they also want more stuff than their neighbour. Consequently, they are always open to receive and buy more stuff and if your product or service is appropriate, they will be open

to the possibility of purchasing it. People very rarely window shop for very long before they decide to buy. If they had no intention to buy at all they wouldn't research or window shop for a moment.

'Make a customer, not a sale'- **Katherine Barchetti**

** Customer Acquisition Cost

The customer acquisition cost is a vital piece of management information and we will cover it in more detail in the reporting section. For now, we will define it as the cost of getting that lead or potential purchaser to the point of sale. This would include any direct marketing costs for instance but should also include some allocation of overheads, possibly staff time and even office costs and management time. This is a calculation task that eventually has to be done because if the cost of acquisition of a customer says £/$20 and the price of the product is only £/$5 then no profit can ever be made. Some business owners are a lot more cautious on the calculation of this cost than others but eventually, we have to know that the cost of getting the customer to the check-out can be covered by the profit within the product itself. In addition, all business costs do have to be covered because even if we make profits on the sale of one product or service there are still many other non-product related costs to pay for.

Top Sales Tips

1. Make sure that the product and its price are clear and simply presented. If your product needs a lot of information here make sure you chunk it into relevant sections allowing the customer to move onto more detail when they are ready. If a product description looks too long or complicated then the customer tunes out and won't buy.

   Trial this with some friends or focus group if you can: identify what information is needed and when more detail needs to be released into the buying process and try to mirror the customer's pace. You know your product well and may consequently be impatient to see how long the customer might need.

   LESS is definitely more in terms of information at the point of sale: but it needs to be enough to enable the customer to justify their buying decision.

2. If you are selling face to face be incredibly knowledgeable about your subject and the product details but keep those details to yourself until asked, or it becomes obvious you need to give more information. What knowledge tends to give you is an air of confidence because you know there's nothing the potential customer can ask that you don't know the answer to, and it makes you relaxed and the sale becomes easier. The customer will sense your ease and relax themselves.

3. Become a great communicator! Develop listening skills and learn to ask the right question and LISTEN to the answer given and take that 'feedback' to determine how to go to the next step. Questioning

the customer is a more relevant step when selling face to face but can be interspersed into any selling process: for instance, partway through a web sale the computer could just pop up and say 'is there anything else you need to know before you click on the button below to go to the shopping basket?'

Web sales are a great way of getting feedback because with sophisticated diagnostics nowadays you can identify when the potential customer drops off the page or how often they click in certain places and so on: this makes it quite easy to then design a sales process that minimises dropouts and gets the customer to the shopping basket in the fewest clicks.

4. Eventually, ask the crucial question and ask for the sale: are you ready to buy this now or do you need to know anything else? I've read some terrifying stats that indicate that up to 85% of salespeople don't actually ever ask for the sale. This is very confusing of the customer – you need to tell them – eventually what you want them to do! They are not mind readers.

5. Ensure that your sales process, and that includes the price, is congruent and consistent with the product. For instance, if you have a cheap product, sell it at a cheap price and in a 'cheap' way such as pile 'em high and sell 'em cheap. Dressing up a cheap product into a fancy one confuses the customer and they go away.

   An expensive product needs to be sold in an expensive way with up lighting, free snacks, personal service and fancy wrapping!

   The product MUST represent fair value, be congruent with the price, and consistent with your chosen branding.

Gill Story

One of the roles that I fulfil in my local area is as the patron of the Chamber of Commerce and in that role, I occasionally go out to business owners to see if I can give any guidance or support.

One of the most common statements I have heard in all my years in performing this type of role is:

"we're going to provide a quality product at a reasonable price".

No, you're NOT!

What a potential customer wants to see is either a quality product at a quality price or a reasonable product at a reasonable price. Confusing the two is a common mistake from a new business owner because there is an element of their thinking that just doesn't believe that any customer would pay a high price for what they are selling.

> *If a quality product is sold at too cheap a price the customer immediately starts to question what's wrong with it. If a reasonable product is sold at a too higher price the customer feels like they are being duped. In either case, nobody wins*

6. In the main, the potential customer makes the decision to buy almost immediately and then spends the rest of their time gathering the evidence to justify their initial, and mainly emotional, decision.

    Apparently, most sales generated from an advert are generated by the headline alone rather than the text that follows. Sales generated from TV advertising happen almost as soon as the advert starts and even in a face-to-face type sale situation the customer will intuitively feel positive - or not - almost immediately. First impressions definitely count here.

    This means you do not have much time to engage with the potential customer and you have to be able to put the information you need right in front of them as quickly as you can.

    Sell on the headline and then justify as you go along. The process needs to be quick and you have maybe only a few seconds before you have lost the customer connection.

7. If your product is not one that can be easily described or presented you may find that the customer needs to see the product displayed many times and tradition tells us that customers need to see information seven times before they buy.

    The seven pieces of information probably need

to be different: an advert, a newsletter, a product flyer, a testimonial, a billboard, some social media commentary and even possibly a lecture or interview given by one of the business managers or owners. These messages endorse you as a business and as a product provider; all of which makes a customer feel happier about buying, particularly if there is some external 'peer' or group input.

The more varied these pieces of evidence are the stronger the picture the potential customer will build about your profile, your business and the product in hand.

This may all sound quite an onerous and lengthy process but if you get your marketing and database management right then many of these 'touchpoints' can happen automatically as soon as the leads are identified and in your world.

The Philosophy of Sales

I want to take a brief moment now to talk about what a sale actually is. It is purely the transfer of a product or service that one person has in their possession to another who has identified a need or want for that particular thing. That's it!

I'm constantly astounded by how negative some people can be towards the sales process and whilst I accept that in some cases you do get a dodgy salesperson or an inadequate product, in the main, there is a fair exchange of goods for cash.

I think it is important for anyone connected with sales, and that is every business owner, to realise that their product is going to fulfil a need that a customer has. If we can identify the customer need early on then it is an easy task to highlight the specific part of your product or service that can fulfil that need. It is possible to be flexible about your product description if you know your customer well enough and you can pick out the parts of the product that you can see the customer wants.

Customers are not victims and hopefully, they will become supporters of your business and product and will enjoy the relationship with you if you manage it properly. Your aim, of course, is to make profits and sell your product but you can do this whilst ensuring you genuinely help the customer and give them something better than they currently have.

There are no losers in a properly managed customer and sales relationship. Your aim is to help and support the customer whilst you gain sales for your business. The more you help your customer the easier that process will be.

Finally, it is worth mentioning that many sales techniques may look manipulative. In the past, I believe this was probably true but is much less so nowadays because any manipulation or negative behaviour on behalf of a sales force for example, would soon be widely distributed information on social media or the web. Consequently, many of the old 'foot in the door' techniques for selling have long gone and have been replaced by more transparent and widely accepted processes.

The trend towards quick, worldwide dissemination of information has resulted in the sales process being a more honest affair, although there are always rogues in any area of life but these are increasingly exposed by both consumer forums and so on and by government bodies, so keep your eye out for those so that you can differentiate your product from theirs if it happens to look similar.

'Most people think 'selling' is the same as 'talking'. But the most effective salespeople know that listening is the most important part of their job.' - **Roy Bartell**

The Sales Arena

There are many different ways that you can get your product in front of a potential customer, and you will need to find the distribution channels that work best for your business and the product you have. They include:

1. A standard **retail shop** where a customer can come in, browse and buy. This can be a high-cost option though as you will either need to buy or rent the shop itself and also invest in fixtures and fittings, staffing and also gain some layout, presentational and window dressing skills.

2. A variant of that may be on a retail park, **factory outlet** or shop in an unusual position (garden centres are particularly good at this in the UK). This tends to be a slightly cheaper cost option for the business owner as you will only pay rent for your little bit of space and you won't have some of the ancillary costs associated with your own shop.

3. Temporary outlets such as food outlets at music

festivals or a '**pop up'** shop at a railway station which clearly are the cheapest method of creating a shop and it's portable too. If you think your product needs to be sold in a shop start with this option first as a test.

4. **Face to face** sales which may happen in a shop but may also happen as a result of an appointment made probably by a lead generation exercise. This is a method used by professionals such as lawyers, accountants, mortgage brokers, will makers, insurance brokers and so on and can be a one-to-one meeting or a one-to-many meeting. This methodology is used by professionals normally because the product they are selling has a high-profit margin or commission element built-in, so it's worth the effort.

The face to face seller needs highly tuned 'closure' techniques which we address later.

5. **Seminar and presentations** explaining or demonstrating your product and this can be anything from a demonstration at an exhibition, to a

talk to say, a local women's group or business forum, and this area also includes specialist seminars during which a speaker normally gives a free couple of hours or so on a particular topic during which the lead is engaged to become a hot prospect or even a sale.

I'm not sure this outlet existed when I started in business but it's very common now and it's easy to attend one of these types of seminars every night of the week in larger cities across the globe.

The types of the product tend to be either high ticket items or the 'professional' sale from lawyers, accountants etc. They also are very popular with education and investment providers.

In fact, I've presented myself at many!

It's an expensive way to sell. Not only have you got the cost of getting the lead in the room you also have the cost of room hire, potentially equipment hire, refreshments and support staff. Conversions also tend to be quite low, and it would be a good guide to assume you have to target at least 10% of the audience to make it work but do your own numbers there.

Also bear in mind that if the seminar is free you get a high proportion of no shows, and I would estimate 50% of your potential audience don't show up so build that into your cost formula!

But then make sure you take that lead and put them into your maintenance funnel and invite them back another time.

6. **On line** which is the largest expanding market place our world has ever experienced and it's covered

in its own section later. This tends to be a cheaper cost to the business than any of the channels listed above.

7. However, the cheapest sale you will ever get is the **repeat sale**! Just imagine if a customer is so happy with what you sell them that they repeat buy on a regular basis where money just bounces into your bank account without any real additional effort from you. In order to achieve this level of comfort from your customer, you need to provide them with appropriate customer care, consistency of product delivery and whatever you do please don't demote these people below your potential new customer.

It is far easier and cheaper to keep an existing customer than it ever is to get a new one.

If you have this happy circumstance with a repeat buy customer, you also have the opportunity of up-selling and cross-selling other products to them as well. Unless you only have one product, a happy customer will naturally be curious about the other things that you provide. You have a clear opportunity and responsibility to provide them with those details and part of your database maintenance routines should be to regularly expose the customer to your other offerings and choices.

A happy customer is also the best salesperson you could have ever have and referrals and recommendations from them are worth their weight in gold. Make sure that you give them the opportunity to provide that feedback on a regular basis, and if necessary, reward them appropriately.

I also want to add at this stage two less familiar sales opportunities.

8. The B2B or **'business to business'** sales activity. So far, we have only concentrated on selling a product to a single retail-type customer but much business nowadays is done at a much higher level between business to another business. If for example, you are a bookseller you have the option of selling your books one at a time through any of the outlets described above but imagine if you sold a thousand books at a time to a supermarket or another bookshop or even to a completely unrelated business such as a healthcare provider who then puts a copy of your book in every one of their customers' pockets.

    In this case, of course, you would have to offer a fairly substantial discount on the price to the other business but that is offset by the vastly reduced costs in getting your product to market. These bulk B2B sales can actually be the method by which you cover your overheads leaving your more profitable individual sales to generate business cash flow and growth.

    Always be on the lookout for places where your product or service could be included in someone else's business enabling them to add value to their particular customer whilst creating sales in your own.

    This technique also has the benefit of getting exposure for your product into a marketplace where your name is not familiar and that enhances your brand and business value, expands your potential sales pool and those customers might just come back to you directly for future purchases.

    I like win-win.

Finally, a weird one:

9. Have you ever thought about doing a deal with your **competitors**? If your competitors have a decent database management regime, they will have a bank of customers who haven't quite bought into their product or service yet. That may be because their particular slant on the product isn't quite what the customer needs or wants - but your version might just be the right match for the customer.

   There are clearly pros and cons to this approach and the disadvantage is that you will be putting money in your competitor's pocket whilst probably revealing detailed information about your product and processes.

   On the other hand, it does enable you to establish another relationship which could be incredibly useful in the future. It could be that between the two businesses concerned you establish a joint-venture arrangement which is beneficial to both parties. For example, one business might be better at product delivery and have cheaper warehousing and storage. The other business might be better at admin and customer care. If you manage to share your joint resources to the effective efficiency of both then I think that's a positive.

   In addition, it tends to be these other businesses where you establish a relationship which becomes the prime prospects when you eventually want to sell your business in its entirety. Trust has already been established and fair value identified. If we go back to our business pyramid, we know that the ultimate aim of any business is for it to be sold and this sales activity and joint-venture activity with another business might just be the way to generate your target lead list for that when happens.

Sales techniques

There are many ways to present your offering to a potential customer but it would be very rare nowadays for the sales proposition to be a simple one of a ticket price which is then readily paid at the checkout. As consumers, we have got used to seeing a variety of deals and discounts and if we don't see some kind of offering at some stage in the sales process there is a sense that there is something missing. Even in some High Street shops, you will find customer haggling at the till for a better deal.

Occasionally, in my own business, we find that potential customers hang around for a while waiting for this better deal to be presented and they won't buy until it is revealed. Of course, sometimes there is no better deal and in which case, we need to manage the customer's expectations of how we can proceed.

Starting with the simplest technique or incentive let's look at some that are routinely used in selling today:

1. Discount for immediate payment, or possibly cash payment. This creates a sense of urgency for the customer but only works if it is a genuine discount at the time. Cash discounts have become less common as we use less cash but this can be replaced with a swipe now option using a debit or credit card.

2. Discounts for multiple purchases where a customer will get cheaper unit price buying two or more of the product. However, the customer needs to be wary here because often the unit price is artificially inflated before the discount is applied and sadly, we see this a lot in supermarket multiple buy offers. My view is that honesty is always the best policy and as soon as the customer feels duped in this way they lose trust and are wary of going forward. As our ultimate dream is to have a continually repeat buying customer then we need to maintain our honesty and integrity as business owners.

3. Combining and adding other products. You see this quite regularly on TV advertorial shopping channel outlets. They start with a brush that does one thing, then they had a bigger brush and yet another brush and each time a brush appears the price gets added to the screen. By the time the entire brush set is revealed the combined screen price is quite high but of course, it is then drastically reduced and then even more products are added such as free cleaning materials, postage and package and so on.

What this technique does is to build perceived value because what starts off as a reasonably priced single brush becomes part of a much greater package at a similar or identical price. The customer clearly feels they have a bargain.

4. Multiple sales which then get unbundled. This method is used generally by businesses where the product price is quite high but where multiple sales could occasionally happen. For instance, let's look at an upmarket expensive ladies clothes shop. A

customer goes into a shop and looks at a variety of dresses. The salesperson approaches the customer and highlights two or three items that the customer has looked at – or even better, tried on - and reveals the price of all three dresses together - let's say £/$1,000. The customer may be able to afford all three and is interested in all three dresses but may feel put off by the price. At this stage, the salesperson then says well £/$1,000 for three, of course, this lovely red dress is only £/$350. By comparison, the £/$350 sounds cheap and affordable and the customer is more ready to buy.

What has happened is that the customer's expectation of expenditure has been raised by the collation of the price of all three dresses together and when the individual price is presented they relax and feel that the cost of the purchase is appropriate, and they're back in their comfort zone and happy to buy.

Of course, the customer may well say they want all three dresses in which case a good salesperson will then start adding accessories to the shopping list such as shoes, bags, hats and jewellery and whatever else the shop has to sell.

5. Trial initial offer or subscription. It is very common when buying a subscription type product or service that there is an initial trial period for say three months where the product is free. Normally the customer is required to enter some financial information such that when the trial period is complete their subscription automatically starts being paid for. A variant of this is the very low-price initial trial period

which then jumps up to the full price later.

This is a very common technique with any product that can be paid for in regular instalments and subscription services are ideal for this technique. I personally just started my second trial offer of Amazon prime because after a while they forget that you have had it! Of course, after three months Amazon will ask me for money again and at that stage, I can make a decision whether the service I've been receiving is worth it.

6. I clearly don't want to give away every secret of Amazon's sales methodologies but it's fairly common knowledge that if you try and cancel, say an audible subscription with them they offer you a reduced monthly rate to stop you from leaving. Many businesses have this immediate price cut if you threaten to cancel or leave and so as a customer, it's worth making that threat from time to time as a matter of policy.

Also, this approach I think does undermine your business and the product or service. If you genuinely believe that your product is worth £/$10 then to discount it to £/$5 for those people that happen to be more assertive makes me feel a little uncomfortable. I much prefer an honest clear price that is applied to all and then there can be no skulduggery. Customers tend not to like it if they feel they are paying more for an equivalent or identical product to another customer and it will make them feel dissatisfied when there was no dissatisfaction in the first place. It seems an unnecessary way to annoy your customers overall so use this technique carefully. It would also only work on fairly low-ticket items.

7. Loss leader items. Supermarkets are fabulous at this particular technique and it's worth going into a supermarket just to see how they present their products for sale. Customers will be lured into the shop with the promise of a few very cheap items that are highly marketed and advertised. Once in the shop customer continues walking round to pick up all their other shopping where the profit margins are much higher. Overall the supermarket wins. They are interested in making a profit overall and quite happy to sacrifice a few pence or cents here and there in order to achieve that larger aim.

In addition to this technique is to offer a discount or a free voucher for a particular item that has to be collected from the store. It would be a very disciplined customer indeed who went to the store for their free item who then walked out with nothing else when they have to walk through the entire shop to get it.

Supermarkets will also place goods strategically throughout the store making sure that any customer has to walk more or less throughout the whole shop before they find what they need. This is the reason that in the UK the bread counters are always at the back of the store because most customers pick up a loaf when they're out shopping.

They will also place sweets and snacks by the till because by the time the shopper gets to check out they are tired and fed up and they crave sugar. In the UK there is now legislation to stop this particular activity.

Finally, a supermarket will place difficult to sell items at eye level on their shelves making sure that the maximum number of people see the product as they wander around. The products that will automatically be bought in a weekly shop will be positioned near the floor or on the top shelves because the store knows that you will make the effort to pick them up anyway.

'How you sell is more important than what you sell.'-
Andy Pail, author, speaker & strategist of Zero-Time Selling

There are a few other techniques that I want to add that are more relevant to the face-to-face type of sale situation:

8. Withdrawing the offer. Occasionally a customer will get into an extremely defensive mode and wouldn't say yes to anything. If the salesperson feels that they have reached an impasse then one technique is simply to say to the customer I don't think this product is for you, I'm sorry you can't have it. As soon as that happens the customer feels affronted because their belief is that they can have anything if they pay the price and they deserve it and qualify for it. At that stage, they start batting for the other side and start demanding to have what they previously decided they didn't want.

   In high ticket items, this is a useful technique to have up your sleeve because genuinely in some businesses you would not want the customer you are being confronted by. Difficult customers reduce profits because you have to spend so much time, effort and potentially money to keep them onside. As a small business owner, you may be desperate for any type of customer but you will regret the day you take on a nuisance. Keep your eye out for these people and be prepared to stand firm and reject the money if you genuinely feel they will cost you more than you earn eventually.

9. Silence is golden. In selling situations many salespeople just talk too much and it's worth remembering that you have two ears and only one mouth.

Some customers just need thinking time to assimilate what you told them and they need the space and silence to do that. Everybody processes at different rates and as a salesperson you need to make sure that you are allowing the customer an appropriate amount of time to do their own processing. They will soon tell you when they need to know more.

10. The 'assumptive' sale which is where the salesperson just automatically assumes that the customer is going to buy. If the salesperson and a potential purchaser have established a very strong relationship over a fairly long period of time then the benefits of the product and all the details about the offering will be well-known and clear between the two parties. In this case when it comes to the closure point of the sale the salesperson can just assume that the purchaser is going ahead and can, for example, start filling out the appropriate paperwork or invoice at that stage.

11. Peer or partner pressure. If you have a couple who are potential purchasers inevitably one will be more positive toward your product than the other and it can be a useful technique to get the more willing partner to help you to sell to the less willing one. Normally a person will have a much greater idea of how to persuade their partner to take action than you, as an independent person, can ever glean from a short sales meeting.

    An extension to this is to get a peer group to sell to each other as each person provides 'social proof' of success or satisfaction to the others. Often a person wants what their peers have in any case and so to be offered a familiar product from a familiar face is an easy sale.

Finally, a crazy little secret from me. My main business places full-page ads in a free newspaper that gets distributed in and around London. These newspapers are often left on trains, in restaurants and cafés as a matter of course. When I'm out in town I open these newspapers to our full-page ad and leave it turned face up back on the seat such that every person that walks by or tries to sit down has our advert clearly in view. This may not generate many sales but makes me feel like I am making the effort as a business owner. After all, we walk around the world one step at a time and if I can create one sale from that simple crazy task then I'm very willing and happy to do it.

***

Gill Story: The wedding dress shop

A couple of years ago my youngest daughter and her best friend were invited to be bridesmaids at a wedding. As a contribution, I agreed to buy their bridesmaids dresses and the bride gave us the details of the dress she wanted them to wear and that included colour, stock code and also the outlet that sold the dress in a bridal shop nearby.

We all duly trundled down to the shop in question, walked in and found exactly the two dresses we needed both in terms of size, colour, code and price. I whipped out my credit card and presented it to the assistant who then looked at it as if it were a piece of litter. "Oh no", she said we can't sell dresses just on the day you have to make an appointment and come in and be measured. I pointed out that the girls had fitted the dresses perfectly but she was adamant that we could not buy the dresses on the spot and that we would have to come back and make an appointment and be properly measured and then she would sell us the dresses once an order had been made.

Suffice it to say we walked out of that shop, found another supplier where we walked in and bought the two dresses we needed in a heartbeat.

It won't surprise you to read that that original wedding dress shop has now gone out of business. I appreciate that they were trying to create a pampering brand where part of the experience was the preamble to the actual purchase which included cups of tea, copious body measurements (presumably to create an up-sale in exact alterations) followed by flicking through brochures and stock items. However, in this case, they had a willing customer, a willing buyer and the money being presented to them on a plate.

There are times when circumventing your standard procedures is essential and any business of whatever size needs the flexibility to cope with the customer in hand. If a customer presents you with a request for a sale then for heaven sake take it!

The lack of flexibility in this particular case led to the entrepreneur losing their business and that's a shame.

Price points

There's a great deal of science and a little twist of mysticism that goes into identifying a product price. Tips that may help are:

1. Keep your product price in line with that of your competitors. The less sensitive your prices the less you need to worry about this but overall customers choose the cheaper price for the identical product if they can.

2. Avoid rounding up. This is why you see so many products priced at £/$599, £/$999 and so on as it sounds so much cheaper than £/$600 or £/$1,000.

3. There was a trend a few years ago to having seven in product prices and I believe this came from some Asian influence. In all honesty, I never noticed any of my products selling more actively if the price had a seven and I suggest this trend soon tired of itself. However, if there is overwhelming evidence in your product arena for a certain number or price point then just take it.

4. Make sure that your price is just fractionally below any legislative, taxation or excise duty limits. For instance, in the UK we have to apply stamp duty on the purchase of assets at certain levels and this duty increases the higher the value of the asset concerned. Keep your price just below any price or percentage band increases.

    In addition, there are different taxes that apply to different product sets and in the UK, for instance, we have IPT (Insurance Premium Tax) that applies solely to insurance products.

There will be different issues at hand for different territories across the globe here and in the US, for example, there may be both state and federal taxes to bear in mind.

Please make sure you check your local territory and the appropriate rules regulations and taxes for your product or service and charge it appropriately.

5. Ideally, prices should be quoted gross of all taxes, duties and charges otherwise the customer gets a little deflated once they get to the checkout and the price increases accordingly. Some countries are much more used to this than others but in the UK the expectation is that the ticket price on the product is the exact price you will pay. In the US customers are much more used to mentally calculating the additional cost of the sales taxes as they shop.

6. In the UK the main sales tax is VAT (Value Added Tax) but not all businesses have to be registered to levy or charge this to a customer. Please check to see if your business has reached the relevant limit or not.

7. There are ways to present the price of the product that makes the customer specifically choose a particular item. With a low price item if you present a range of products at varying prices then the customer will inevitably choose the cheapest one. This enables the business owner to deliberately present prices to drive the customer to the product that the salesperson ideally wants them to take. All you have to do is to put your ideal price item cheapest and then add on top slightly more sophisticated or alternative, more expensive products, which the

customer will then duly ignore. And if they happen to buy the more expensive product well that's a bonus.

With more expensive products a customer tends to buy the middle price because that feels comfortable and safe. They have avoided the cheap option but they have also held back from spending top dollar. Again, a business owner can deliberately present products and product ranges in order to drive the customer to the product and the price they want.

There is a lot of psychology attached to human behaviour and purchasing and although most of it may be common sense, please watch other businesses (especially big ones) who may have done a lot more research in this area than you can afford when you're a small entity.

Profitability

Ultimately what any business owner wants is a profitable product and a profitable business and any business owner needs to get a firm grasp on what they believe their potential profit percentage could be.

As a rough rule of thumb, I always take a 10% profit per annum and that is net of all costs. To calculate the different levels of profit what you do is to take your sales price and deduct the direct cost of sale of the product to create your ***gross*** profit percentage. This percentage may be quite high. Then you deduct all the other costs of getting your product to market including overheads and ancillary costs and anything that you spend and that will leave you with a much smaller number and a much smaller **net** profit percentage. This is the net profit percentage of 10% that I measure.

Please don't exclude some costs as not being relevant - **every** cost is relevant to the business and at the end of the day those costs need to be paid from product sales

There are huge amounts of statistics out there that will give you a better guide to the profitability of your specific industry or business type.

Here is a chart showing the net rates of return for the UK privately owned and non-financial companies.

United Kingdom

	Net rates of return of UK Private Non-financial Companies (%)
2007	11.4
2008	11.4
2009	9.7
2010	10.8
2011	11.4
2012	11.2
2013	11.2
2014	12.0

Source: Office for National Statistics

You will see that my approximate guide of 10% per annum is a realistic one compared to actual profitability for standard businesses in the UK. These figures have been calculated by the UK ONS (Office for National Statistics) who will also provide specific profitability figures for different industries in different marketplaces.

Other territories will have information for their own

country so please click around the Internet to find something relevant for you.

As a business owner, these general national statistics also provide you with a target and a comparison. Use them to monitor your performance and to provide you with objectives to meet. If you constantly fall behind what your competitors are doing then clearly you are doing something wrong. These figures might give you the vital feedback that business ownership is not for you, or at least give you the incentive to get help.

Sales and the economy

However carefully you market your product and identify accurate price points there are times when a product just will not sell. There are many reasons for this: it may have passed its sell-by date or your product may have fallen behind that of your competitors. In both cases you probably can do something about it, however, sometimes you just have to change your product to fit the external world.

There is evidence to show that product prices and product types need to be changed in changing economic environments. When an economy is booming then certain products become fashionable and demand increases. There's a marketing adage in the UK that suggests that the stronger the economy the shorter skirt lengths tend to be, which may help those businesses in the fashion industry.

The economic expansion also tends to lead to higher demand for luxury products and health-related products because the economic buoyancy results in an individual customer feeling good about themselves and wanting to reward themselves a little more.

Conversely, we also have evidence that in times of economic restriction people eat more and the reason given for this is that when people feel unhappy with the economic news they comfort eat. If your product is stodgy puddings like mum used to make then this is your time!

Furthermore, when times are hard 'retro' products tend to do well as customers look to the good old days to cheer themselves up.

Think about how you can adapt your products, and the product prices, to changing economic environments and the longer you're in business the more you will see this happen and you can be prepared for it.

Bundling and unbundling

One way that you can cope with the changing economic environment is to create a product set that you can bundle together and then unbundle at another time.

Imagine that you produce kits to make celebration cakes. In boom times that can be a complete package including the cake, the cake board, decorative items, a cake knife, matching serviettes, matching tablecloths, cake forks, presentation boxes and invitations. You could sell these as your special wedding kit, birthday kit, anniversary kit, graduation kit and so on. There is also the opportunity to add ancillary services and products to these kits.

But then when the economy turns you just take all the

individual items listed above and sell them individually, and you could even sell the recipe for the cake itself. What you have done is turned a high ticket item into a selection of low priced products which you can hopefully sell even though the market is tight and this technique alone may be enough to get you through the tough times and until the economy turns.

My rule of thumb is that when an economy is contracting, I go for basic or vanilla products and when an economy is expanding, I go for the full bells and whistles and the gold-plated version.

Now apply those techniques!

Having now looked at sales in general we can now go back the strategic pyramid and start combining that with the specific techniques needed for each size of business.

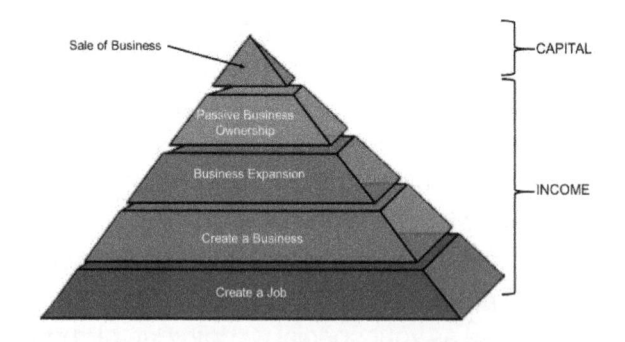

It would be very unusual for any new business to start anywhere other than the bottom two, or possibly bottom three tiers, of this pyramid.

Most businesses start with a solitary entrepreneur

who is creating a living for themselves rather than having a job. In this case, the sale is based purely on the skills of that business owner and s/he might already have a customer base derived from the previous employment. In this case, there is a ready-made customer list and the sales relationship is very much a personal and face-to-face one.

Even if this lone entrepreneur does not have a ready bank of customers, at this stage the sale very much comes from the business owner and they need to get very public with their offering in some shape or form.

Some sales techniques listed will be more obvious and a more appropriate match to what the business does. However, don't be afraid to borrow a technique from the sector of the marketplace that traditionally your product doesn't fit in. We learn more from expanding beyond our comfort zone and by exploration than we ever do by standing still.

It is likely that, whatever size the business is, it will need a variety of sales approaches and you will eventually combine some or all of the above.

If yours is a very personal service such as coaching or mentoring then you will sell on the strength of your ability, and probably referrals. If your product is a generic widget type industry then your ability or reputation has very little to do with anything.

However, the principles remain true. Your aim is to get your customer buying, and then repeat buying with ease and confidence and whatever you can do in order to make that paradise happen is the business owners main task. Whatever works when the business was small will probably continue to work as it grows and expands up the strategic pyramid.

Even the largest supermarkets across the globe generally started with one corner shop or a market stall and as the business became more successful a second shop was opened and so on until thousands of outlets exist across the world. The principle remains the same and the sales proposition and the way that it is delivered is identical in a massive hyper store as it is in a tiny shop.

Firstly, a customer has to be driven into that distribution outlet in some way and that happens with the marketing. Then the customer has to be shown a selection of products and the relevant prices: they need to be teased with a discount or an offer and then reassured about product cost, value and delivery.

Of course, these techniques get very much more sophisticated if we are dealing with Walmart or IKEA but the theory remains constant and any small store can use all the same incentives and motivations as the larger ones. The main difference is that the larger stores have economies of scale and may be able to offer larger discounts or incentives but what the smaller store has is the benefit of more personalised customer care and attention.

Therefore, if your chosen method of sales is via a retail shop then as you grow up the business pyramid and expand, you just open more shops - and bigger ones!

If your product involves face-to-face selling, such as a professional service, you just need to get more 'faces' as the business grows.

And amazingly, if you sell via the web or in the virtual world in any way, then once you have identified the route of the 1st sale then that route holds true for the 1,000th sale or even for the 1,000,000th sale.

Therefore, once you have mastered the sales

techniques that work for your product or service, it is likely that those same techniques will serve you all the way up the business strategic pyramid until you eventually sell the business, and those techniques, to somebody else.

A fledgling entrepreneur or small business owner need not be afraid of sales as there is nothing magical that the larger organisations know that the smaller organisation can't replicate.

All businesses of all sizes have only one objective: getting the customer to put the product into their shopping cart to buy is the overriding and number-one objective.

Finally, be prepared to change. The marketplace and times are constantly changing and, in my business lifetime the general sales trend has gone more or less from face-to-face selling to virtual sales

In the UK we have seen the demise of the local high street, for example, as the local retail shop has been overtaken by the larger retail parks and even those are now under threat from the Internet.

What worked for you in the past is unlikely to keep working for you in the future and the pace of change is increasing, therefore, it is absolutely crucial that you continually test your sales techniques and their effectiveness constantly.

> *'Listen to your customers deeply, or you will have none.'* -
> **Bryan Clayton, CEO of Greenpal**

Testing, Testing

When you first start your business there are two tests to complete: firstly, testing your competitors' sales methodologies and then testing your own. How easy is it to actually buy either their product or your own? I'm constantly amazed when I try to buy goods at how complicated and difficult some organisations seem to make the process. I shudder with horror when I enter some retail shops for example because the stock is so cluttered and crammed in that even if you wanted to buy something it would be almost physically impossible to get the stock off-the-shelf or the rack (dress shops are major culprits of this!).

As a business owner, you have the responsibility of making sure that your customer's journey to the checkout is as simple, easy and painless as possible. Unfortunately, your staff won't have quite the same passion for this as you.

Then once you are relatively clear on your process then you need to check in from time to time to make sure that it still works. That can be done by you as the business owner but as you expand your business this won't necessarily be a great use of your time and in any case, you will soon easily be recognised.

Therefore, you need to engage some mystery shoppers of some kind to go through your sales process with a critical eye and give you the feedback.

Mystery shopping is quite an established and growing business of itself these days and every organisation of any size should be making sure that they are receiving independent feedback about their sales journey such that they can constantly improve the flow. Also make sure that all parts of the sale cycle are tested: from lead generation, direct sales process plus the essential aftercare.

Conclusion: Sales

At the end of the day what you are looking for is the cheapest and most effective and most profitable way to get your product in front of a potential customer so that they can buy it, and you may not discover that immediately. What you thought was the ideal way to sell your product may turn out to not work for your business model and I encourage you to do some testing early on as to what works and what doesn't.

If in doubt start at the cheapest point and work your way up to the more expensive distribution methods as you go but be prepared to be proved wrong by the reality of your sales. It is important not to carry too many preconceived ideas into your business as things change very fast and you may just be outdated. Also, be prepared to change as you grow your business - what was a perfect sales outlet last year may just have become out of date today.

Furthermore, you may just have to sacrifice something to get your sales to close. Certainly, at the beginning you may have to give away a little more until you get an established business with an established, trusting client base that you can then grow.

Finally, I'm afraid to say that it is not always the best product or service on the market that becomes the market leader. The product that is marketed best, sold in the easiest way for the customer and supported by an appropriate customer care function will be the product that wins even though here are better alternatives on the market. Your product may still fail even if it's the 'best' one!

The product itself is vitally important but if no potential customer knows where it is or ever gets to see it then it's worthless.

C. After the Sale

Even after a sale - or proposed sale - the marketing efforts need to continue and never stop. Marketing has many tasks and that includes reputation building and profile maintenance. Any contact or customer that you connect with will check out your profile, your credentials, the business profile, the website as well as any and all reviews posted or written about you to make sure you're who you say you are and to check the validity of your business and offerings. A word of warning here - they may even check out all your personal stuff so be careful of what you post on your social media channels as that needs to fit with your business too. People want to see that you don't suddenly become a lunatic privately as that suggest a lack of judgement and congruency.

Where can marketing continue to help?

Your website:

Whatever your business there are some essentials needed that will ensure your website is optimised to be user friendly and therefore in the best position to make a sale.

Below is a handy checklist:
1. Does your website have logical navigation? Is it easy for a customer to find what they are looking for and more importantly is there a

clear path to purchase.

2. Make sure it's clear who you are and what you're selling. It's obvious to you but being clear on these things will let your customer know what you're all about and why they should become your customer.

3. Include your contact information!

4. Security is a big thing so, make sure your website has an SSL Certificate.

5. Integrate your social media; customers expect to see the icons and to be able to click directly through to your social pages.

6. Test your website on mobile, is it mobile friendly? Does it render correctly or look a bit squiffy?

7. FAQ is a quick and easy way to address a customer's questions, fears and scepticism.

8. There's nothing worse than a website that doesn't load quickly. Slow load times result in customers walking away.

9. And finally, and this rule applies to all your marketing platforms. Make sure you have a strong CTA (Call to Action), tell the customer exactly what they have to do, such as 'click here to buy'. The more you can craft your sales messages and CTA's the more success you will have when it comes to conversion.

Your CRM System/ Platform:

You have now connected to a customer and they can now become part of your database and you can continue, and enhance, the relationship.

It's natural to say 'thank you' to your customer for accepting your services or purchasing your products and online should be no different. That gratitude can be built within your newly set up CRM system.

There will be how-to-guides for your CRM system that will take you through the process step by step and you should look to integrate this with your website. Once a sale has gone through, acknowledge the sale with an email that says 'thank you – it'll be sent through or we'll be in contact soon'. You can also continue the follow-up and email asking for a review, a follow-on social media or showing them other things that they might be interested in because of their original purchase. Upselling to a current customer is a lot easier than selling to a brand new one.

Think about your campaigns and processes, how can you build an effective sales funnel that will keep your customer happy and buying.

Getting Reviews:

Work on getting your review numbers up and achieving a 5* rating. The more reviews and the higher your star rating the more likely a customer will trust you and make a purchase. There are plenty of ways to get reviews for free, simply ask customers who have purchased your product or service to leave you a review on any of the below:

- Facebook Recommendations and Reviews
- Linked-In Recommendations, Skills & Endorsements
- Google reviews
- Amazon Customer Reviews

If you offer a trade, there's www.ratedpeople.com and if you have the budget, invest in a platform such as www.trustpilot.com where you can ask for reviews by sending a simple email from the platform itself or by building it into your sales funnel.

Spot a review from a happy customer, use that to endorse your products and use it as a testimonial on your website or social media. Reviews inspire trust and confidence in your products and services, so why not showcase a happy customer's experience and prove that your business delivers exactly what it says on the tin!

Now you might be wondering about negative reviews. This isn't something to shy away from but an opportunity to turn that negative into a positive, if they had a bad experience don't get defensive but apologise, offer a refund or offer to discuss how you can improve their experience. A negative review is a chance to learn if something isn't quite going to plan and gives you the opportunity to fix it.

It's worth noting that the internet is an easy gateway for customers to voice their opinions and sometimes this can be in the form of angry comments – don't take it to heart! Do the best you can, with your customer service hat on, to appease them and move on if a resolution isn't possible – it could very well be they are just having a bad day!

Word of Mouth:

Word of mouth is quite possibly the cheapest and most effortless form of marketing. It doesn't require you to do anything if a customer has had a positive experience and if you, as a business, have gone above and beyond, the chances are that that customer who received the good service will tell their friends, family and colleagues who in turn may become customers.
Easy right!

'Marketing is really just sharing your passion'- **Michael Hyatt, NY Times Best Selling Author**

D. Social Media and the Virtual World

Now, social media is a biggie for any SME! It will be the cheapest method of marketing and way of raising awareness of your brand, so it's important to get it right straight away. For this reason, here is a step-by-step guide to setting up your social media pages.

Getting Started:

When beginning your social media journey, the first essential step before selecting your social media channels is to identify and understand who your target audience is, and how they interact online, to best determine which social media channels would be the most beneficial for reaching and engaging with them.

However, the extent to which you invest in social media is completely up to you.

To do this, you will need to segment your audience into the categories below to best guide your channel selection and content creation. You should be able to do this easily by visiting your marketing strategy.

- *Geographic*: Where is your target audience located?
- *Demographic*: What is the size and value of your audience by their gender and age?
- *Behaviours*: Once you have an outline of your target audience based on their criteria, it is key to analyse their online activities to understand how they are using social media, what channels they are on and how they interact.
- *Psychographic*: Lastly, how are you going to know that your target audience is interested in what you have to offer? Knowing your audience's interests is essential.

This next section is a complete guide to social media platforms. We have changed the font so you can easily find this guide when you need to reference back. This section is also available as a useful aide-memoire on our site www.businessforwealth.com.

FACEBOOK:

Facebook is regarded as the social media giant, with the largest number of users ranging from commercial to personal use. This, combined with the special features of creating a business/public page, setting up events, paid advertisement etc, makes it the perfect platform to set up your own page.

Setting up a page

Setting up a public page on Facebook is easy and can be done in less than five minutes. The benefits of creating a page are that it forms a professional look and feel, and it solidifies the legitimacy of your network. Furthermore, it acts as a medium for reaching and interacting with the public through likes, follows, shares and comments. This is a great tool to use in order to best grow your network's profile.

PLEASE NOTE: When creating your page DO NOT set up the account as a private personal profile, this will need to be set up as a business page.

From here you can set up a private group or an event for your business too.

@mentions

If you want to call out another public Facebook page or user, you can directly link to their Facebook page, which also notifies them that you're talking about them, by putting an @ and then typing their name (Facebook will help your selection with a drop-down).

Hashtags

Alongside @mentions there is the hashtag #, by using this tool you can improve the likelihood of your content being viewed as you improve its searchability. Unlike Instagram, on Facebook, it is good practice to limit yourself to 2-5 hashtags per post as anymore looks unprofessional.

Be sure to use a couple to enhance your reach.

Message

People can send your page private messages. You'll find that most of these messages will be customer service-related, so make sure to check them. The message section functions as an email inbox.

Notifications

The notifications box will show you the most recent likes, comments, wall posts, etc., on your brand's page. Depending on the volume of incoming activity, this administrative section can be useful when tracking activity by your community. Due to Facebook's focus on recent activity, you'll probably only receive comments and likes on recent posts, but the notifications can help track activity on older posts.

Facebook Insights

A great way to gain insight into how well your page and content is performing is by using Facebooks built-in system 'Facebook Insights'. This tool provides you with highly valuable data on your audience and your best performing content.

INSTAGRAM

Perfect for photos, Instagram continues to go from strength to strength. Facebook acquired Instagram a couple of years ago which means sharing content between the two platforms is easier than ever before. By combining forces you can increase your exposure.

Setup

Instagram is a mobile app so you will have to download the platform from your mobile app service. It is very straightforward to register with Instagram, simply register with an email address and create a username and away you go. You will notice that upon registering, your account will be set as public, I'd recommend you keep it on this setting as people will be able to see and find you outside your current network.

Now that you have your privacy settings set, you can upload your profile picture, we suggest either your logo or a professional photo of yourself, either way, make sure the account is recognisable to your users. Alongside the profile picture, you can also add a 150-character bio, which is a short description of your business, your location, and your website link.

Notifications

As identified, Instagram is a mobile app, therefore you can receive notifications directly to your mobile. This is great if you want to keep up to date with your followers and reply to any questions your followers may have. If you decide to turn off your Instagram notifications, you will still be able to access updates when you log back into your Instagram account.

Connecting with other Social Media accounts

A great feature of Instagram is that you can link up your account with other social pages such as Facebook and Twitter. By doing so you can easily and more effectively share content from one channel to the other.

Photos and Editing
Instagram revolves around sharing photos. To do this, click the camera button and this will automatically activate your mobile's camera, in this mode you can choose to take a photo or select an existing one from your camera reel.

When uploading an existing image to Instagram keep in mind that it will automatically crop the image to a square, so don't forget to resize the image while in the uploading stage. At this stage you can also edit your image, by using Instagram's iconic feature of filters and borders, here you can create effects to get that professional look!

On top of these features, Instagram also provides tools such as Boomerang and a multi-slider slideshow to create unique and engaging imagery. To add a Boomerang to your feed, you will need to download the Boomerang app.

Video

With Instagram video, you can record short video clips ranging anywhere from three to sixty seconds long. You can also choose to film either one continuous segment or several clips spliced together, which allows for some creative stop motion or animated videos.

Sharing

Once your video/photo is ready to go, you will be sent to the social sharing page. Within this section, you can add a description, your location, hashtags # as well as the ability to tag people in your post via @mention, this works well for increasing your reach particularly if you plan on sharing across to Twitter.

Next, you can choose which networks you have linked to so that you can send the content over to the other channels.

Instagram also allows you to share content from other accounts, however, to do this you will require the app Repost, which will allow you to download the photo/video and will also credit the owner.

Instagram Stories

Instagram Stories are temporary videos or photos that are strung together to form a slideshow gallery that lasts for 24hours. This is a fantastic feature that allows you to tell a story to your users. You can quickly launch Stories by swiping right from the main screen. Within Stories, you can choose to start a live stream, share photos and videos, or create a Boomerang. You can also edit your content with text or add a drawing by selecting the pen tool.

Follow Users

Of course, like other social channels, you can follow other users. We suggest looking for those that you would like to have at your event and begin to build up a rapport with them to build a connection.

Monitoring
We suggest converting your Instagram account into a business account. To do this, you will require a Facebook page. By linking your Facebook and Instagram accounts, you will be able to sync your data from both accounts into Instagram insights (similar to Facebook insights) this tool will enable you to make strategically better content. You can also see basic analytics within your Instagram App, however, this is easier to view on your computer.

TWITTER

A favourite for celebs and businesses, Twitter provides a platform for microblogging 280-character tweets. Twitter is great for interacting with other users through its unique ability to tweet and retweet content.

Signing Up

To sign up you will need to create a handle, this is your Twitter address that should quickly describe who you are. By creating a handle users can interact with you through

@mention for example 'Great time @yourbusiness.

Furthermore, your profile pic, header image and bio should also reflect who you are. You should use your actual picture or business logo alongside your real name, so people feel more comfortable interacting with you.

Start Following

At first, when you open your account, Twitter's algorithm doesn't know you very well, so can't make any tailored suggestions for you. To start this off, begin following a selection of users such as industry professionals and businesses in the fields you're interested in networking with. Once you begin doing this, Twitter will start to make suggestions based on your follows. We also suggest following your local business leaders to build your portfolio in your territory.

Before you start following others, it is good practice to start tweeting interesting content, so when you begin to follow other users, the chances of them following you back is increased.

Engaging with others

By using @mention and inserting a handle you can tag a person into your conversation. By clicking 'view conversation' on a tweet this will display all the responses a message receives, including tweets from people you aren't following. You can see when someone follows or @ mentions you in the Connect tab.

By adding a # you can trend along with trending topics which can assist with increasing your chances of reaching your desired audience. You can also make your own hashtags depending upon your topic of discussion.

Retweeting

Retweeting is an excellent way of getting your tweets shared across Twitter, and it is the best way to get your information spread virally to large numbers of people, so don't be afraid to use those # and @!

Photos and Videos

On Twitter, you can share photos, videos, and website links. The most engaging content on social media includes an image or film attached. However, don't go overboard, be wise and get the balance of image and text right, especially when using Twitter. Unlike Facebook and Instagram, Twitter is still largely text-based.

Linking with other social networks

As discussed with most social media channels there is the option to integrate your networks. For example, you can sync Twitter with Instagram and LinkedIn.

Linkedin

LinkedIn works by providing you with a platform to network with other business professionals and companies. This channel will be an essential tool for building valuable connections for your business.

Setting up your profile

LinkedIn is a personal profile that is made up of your career/business experience and professional skills. It is crucial to complete your entire profile to the fullest (and truthfully). Alongside having accurate information about yourself, your profile picture should be one that reflects professionalism and of course yourself. So, make sure to upload a picture that is recent, clear and presentable.

Uploading documents

While creating your profile, LinkedIn has a great feature that allows you to upload documents. This is a great tool to use for advertising your business, or for uploading important documents for your members.

Boosting awareness

LinkedIn rewards profiles that are complete, by providing a "profile strength" from 0-100%. The higher the rate the higher the chances your profile will appear in search results.

Making connections

LinkedIn is all about making connections. Once you have created your profile, it's time to start connecting. Connecting works by adding people you know. LinkedIn will ask to access your email contacts and send an email asking them to connect on your behalf. By connecting with people you know, you will find that they will endorse your skills, this is an important activity as it adds credibility to your profile, so it is worth connecting!

When you have made more connections, (and have been creating and sharing content), now is the time to begin connecting with other professionals who you would like to see your products and invite to your events.

Sharing Content

In comparison to other social channels, LinkedIn content is tailored around industry and professionals. There are various locations where you can source content that you can share across to LinkedIn, whether it's from LinkedIn itself or across the web.

Of course, you can make your own content by simply typing in the messaging box. In this box, you will see the options that allow you to post links, photos and even articles, which are unique to LinkedIn.

Just like Facebook, Instagram and Twitter, you can @ mention and Hashtag #, however like Facebook it is best practice to limit the number of hashtags you use per post to 2-5.

Connecting with Twitter

As highlighted, you can link both your Twitter and LinkedIn accounts. The benefits of doing this are that you can combine both your networks follower data and, also post tweets through to your LinkedIn account. What is great about this, is that users on your LinkedIn can interact with your tweets, just like on Twitter by retweeting and favouriting.

Whatsapp

WhatsApp is a free mobile messaging app. Within the app, you can set up group chats where you can share messages, images, audio and video. This is a great way to keep connected with your network and with other networking leaders. WhatsApp is available to download on both Android and iPhone.

Learn more at https://www.androidcentral.com/whatsapp

Now you're set to grow your followers and attract customers to your business!

Remember the saying 'content is king' and make sure you stay on the brand so no matter where a customer sees you, they will recognise that its you.

SMM (Social Media Marketing)

Posting on social media can be very effective in spreading the word throughout your personal network, however, you are limited to your network.

Paid advertising through platforms such as Facebook and Instagram is now easier than ever and perfect for promoting your business.

Paid Social Media

Facebook:

Once you have created your advertisement you can 'boost' it. By boosting your post, product or event you can target people that you are not directly in contact with. This enables you to choose what kind of people you would like to see your product or be at your event and by using Facebook's targeting tool, you can strategically decide whether you want to target the audience you defined in your planning or if you would like to target everyone in a certain area or even people with certain interests.

You can learn more here: https://www.facebook.com/business/products/ads

Instagram:

Alongside Facebook, you can also run your advertisements via Instagram and sync them with your Facebook page, which is another great way to increase your exposure! You can promote your business using images, video, carousels (flicking multiple images) or even through your stories.

To learn how to advertise using Instagram visit: https://business.instagram.com/advertising

Linked In:

LinkedIn is your professional platform, with over 610M active professionals. You can select a unique audience based on your initial planning and demographics research and/ or target an audience based on job title, function or industry. Ads are easy to set up and the budget easy to control, you can even take advantage of the direct messenger function and go straight to your target audience's inbox.

If LinkedIn is right for your audience and business, learn how to market to them here: https://business.linkedin.com/marketing-solutions/ads

Twitter:

Likewise, Twitter is another platform where you can advertise, much like Facebook and LinkedIn in that you can easily upload your content, tailor your target audience, control your budget and analyse your campaign results.

To get started on Twitter, take a look at this useful guide: https://business.twitter.com/en/solutions/twitter-ads.html

YouTube:

If you have a collection of videos you can use them to advertise using YouTube. Over the past two years, the number of SMEs who are using YouTube as an advertising platform has doubled! It's also the second most used search engine with on average users spending 30mins a day on the platform. Now those are big numbers, so as an SME why not get involved!

You can learn how to advertise on YouTube here: https://www.youtube.com/intl/en-GB/ads/

Scheduling and Analysing Social Media:

I can appreciate there's a lot to take on board here, remembering the different passwords for everything is chore enough! So, if you're worried that you'll need to be signing in and out of different platforms constantly to add content, don't worry about that either, there's a couple of tools that can help you out.

The two most popular platforms are www.SproutSocial.com and www.Hootsuite.com. Both offer you, the user, the ability to schedule in your posts and see how well your post has performed. You can also 'listen' to your competitors and see what they are doing by selecting their feeds and adding them to your dashboard.

Hootsuite is free to use, whereas Sprout Social offers 30 days free followed by a subscription. That might be the decider for you depending on the budget!

As with finding the right CRM tool for you and your business I'd recommend you do your due diligence, talk to the sales team and ask to see a demo. Makes sure it's the right system for you and your business needs!

Another handy tip, like emails, is to put yourself in your customers' shoes, how often do you think they want to hear from you? There is plenty of guidance out there so do a bit of research and see how often you should post and what time is best to post as these differ from platform to platform.

Creative Tools:

There's no doubt about it, Social Media is HUGE! Luckily there are numerous platforms out there to help us business owners create attractive design work to post on our pages and attract customers. A few of the best are:

Canva:

Canva will become your best friend! It's free to sign up to with the option of signing up to a business account if you need more. It has free images, templates and pre-set size guides for all your needs, and that includes anything from your social media posts to creating flyers and attractive letterheads. You can also save your brand colours, so they are always there and upload your own imagery!
www.canva.com

Bannersnack:

Earlier we looked at display and banners, and you can create these in Canva, but Bannersnack is a much easier tool to use if you want to make moving display banners. It dubs itself the most powerful banner maker on the web, and we believe them! It's free to sign to join, includes templates, guides and you can download the files in whichever format you need and use this across your website, social and through your Google Advertising for example.
www.bannersnack.com

Biteable:

Another free platform to sign up to, Biteable hosts 85,000+ real-life Shutterstock clips and animations, from here you can select the video that best suits your brand and supports your messaging. There is also a huge selection of templates so you can give video creation a go if you would like.
www.biteable.com

Bixabay:

Stuck for photography? Bixabay allows you to select and download royalty-free images to use in your marketing. Sign up for free and bring your content to life with free imagery.
www.bixabay.com

Shutterstock and iStock Photo:

If you have a little more budget it might be worth splashing out on one of these subscription packages. Both include professional photography that you can purchase at a low cost.
www.shutterstock.com or www.istockphoto.com

Now you have the tools, let's get started on creating some show-stopping creative that will really make your business stand out!

You can use these tools to create 'freebies',

newsletters, update your email campaigns with eye-catching headers and 'thumb-stopping' social media content.

Next let's look at the types of things you can do to attract more customers, get more leads and increase your database.

Freebies:

Give something away for free! This may sound counterintuitive but if you are able to create anything that showcases your experience from a book to a simple guide and give it away this will be beneficial to your business in several ways, such as:

1. If you give away a book, your book will be sitting on that person's bookshelf, you'll be in their living room. When they read it, they'll be able to see your experience, they'll remember your name, they may tell a friend about your book, google you... and so the process begins.

2. Similarly, you can create a free guide and place this on your website. To receive the guide, I'd recommend making an exchange, ask for their name and email address. It's a win-win the customer will get a free guide and you'll be able to add them to your database and contact them in the future.

Newsletters:

Like the free guide, this is an exchange. You collect details and in return you give useful information about the business, products and services. It is the easiest and cheapest way to get new leads into your database, so if you don't have a newsletter sign up box integrated into your website, get one. Even if you're not ready to send a newsletter just yet, you'll have a pot of customers waiting to hear from you.

You can create your newsletter using a template in your CRM system or if you're feeling creative in Canva. Newsletters should include updates about your business, what's new, what's exciting, what has 'lit' up your business recently, advertise your product or service and add a testimonial. This is your opportunity to showcase your business, and people like to hear the personal stories from the brands they love.

Remember you don't want to inundate your database's inboxes so try limiting your newsletter to monthly or quarterly and bear in mind if you are sending any other emails you don't want to clash and send two in one day for example.

Webinar:

Depending on your business offering and model, you might consider running a free webinar to generate new leads or give something back to your current database and customers.

www.zoom.com and www.gotowebinar.com are two free services that you can sign up for (business packages are available) and they will allow you to set up a new event and provide you with a link to send out. These platforms also provide analytics so you can go back and see just how well it performed down to how long people watched for.

A webinar is a great opportunity for you to talk more personally with your customers or potential customers. Again, people love to hear personal stories, so start there, introduce yourself, your business, why you're doing what you're doing and introduce your product with the aim of making a sale and do a Q&A at the end to show you're accessible and there for the customer. Use a webinar as a chance to meet new people and connect with your customer.

Live Event Speaking:

Now, I know by this point you're probably exhausted! So, take this as an opportunity to step out from behind your screen and get out there.

Have you ever been to an event with speakers and wondered how they got that gig? Simple, the speakers most likely have one of these qualities. They are an expert in their field, they have an undeniable passion for the work they do and want to inspire others and/or they can offer a product or service that really will make a difference.

There's a mix of paid and free speaking opportunities, ideally, we want to be in the latter category and not pay to use the platform. Research local or nationwide events that have speaking slots and reach out via phone or email to see if they'd be interested in letting you have the stage. If you tick all the three boxes above, the process will be easy. Just remember to keep at it, keep networking and it'll pay off!

Podcasts:

Podcasting has been around since the '80s but only really kicked off in a big way from '04. Nowadays it's bigger than ever, with even more platforms to listen on and, of course, easily accessible as it's all there on your mobile phone.

So why not give your customers another reason to love you and your business. If you've got the right equipment and some editing skills, you can start up your own podcast! However, if this is a little too far out of your comfort zone, how about approaching others to see if they would like to interview you about your business? And in return, you can promote their podcast.

Finally you've now got all the tips and tools to really make your marketing a success! I can't wait to see what you do.

'To continue winning the internet marketing game, your content has to be more than just brilliant- it has to give the people consuming that content the ability to become a better version of themselves.' - **Michelle Stinsonross, Managing Director or Marketing Operations, Apogee Results**

CUST

OMER

(needs to be at the centre of everything you do.)

PROCESS

Processes

The processes in any business can be divided into two areas: the systems (or product or service), and the people to run those systems.

This section will cover both those areas:

A. The systemisation process

Many solopreneurs do not get the point of systemising their processes. As far as they see it, they are a one-man band and they are the system and the system is them and that's as far as it goes

However, the systemisation of the business is vital even at this one wo/man band level as it focuses the mind and gives a solid structure on which to build the business. No business owner wants their business to remain static and a process-driven business is one that has the ability to expand even if that's not the immediate objective of the owner. A system-driven approach to business provides not only the structure or skeleton on which each business process can be hung but also ensures that the business owner approaches their business with professionalism and discipline. This in itself should ensure a higher probability of success.

It's also worth noting that any good system will be able to replicate the business (with the exception of leadership) and that immediately gives the business a level of security and sale-ability. The ultimate aim is that the business system grows alongside the business itself until the system can be independent and become a business all of its own.

Even if you intend never to grow very large as a business, systemisation still pays off and will give you something to sell when you want to stop. It's a tragic shame that many people work in their business and much of their effort goes to waste as they don't systemise it, and have nothing to see at the end of it.

The initial framework

Even when your business is very small there are certain tasks that you need to undertake and they are:

- Sales (to include Marketing and PR),
- Delivery of the product or service (and includes running the shop, or restaurant or delivering the service: coaching, consultancy, whatever),
- Record keeping to include accounts, HMRC, government and whatever you need to report and to whom – and finally
- Strategy, leadership and planning.

This is a good basic structure and even a huge business can still work within this framework but of course, with a large business each of these subdivisions will be broken down into a myriad of other departments and each role such as marketing may have many hundreds of people fulfilling the task.

But let's start first of all with the smallest of businesses and at the bottom tier of our business pyramid.

Someone who has just finished employment to start their own business may have done so because of the passion for their product or service. Unfortunately running your own business has to embrace much more than that and a new business owner has to very quickly acquire a myriad of skills.

An easy tip for any new business owner is to systemise their processes!

One way to do this is to take the four broad categories of business input required and allocate time each week to do each of them. A new business owner will naturally have a liking for one area over the other three but all areas need to be embraced and incorporated otherwise the business has no future at all.

I've seen small business owners break their diary into four separate areas, so for instance marketing is done on Tuesday, record-keeping on Friday and so on. What really helps with this is to place yourself in different places or frameworks. Wear a baseball cap when you're doing the marketing tasks and do them from your office at home. Wear a formal suit when you're doing the record-keeping and pretend that you're an accountant sitting at a posh desk. Whatever works for you in splitting these tasks and getting you into the right frame of mind to do them, is what you need to do otherwise your liking for one of the strands of the business will just overtake you and absorb all the time you have. The peril with that approach is that sooner or later you will need to generate a new sale for instance or submit a tax return, when you've done no preparation.

It makes sense to create time and space for each of the four areas to be covered appropriately and if the business is divided systematically in this way then if appropriate, one whole strand of the business or part of the business strand can be allocated to an external resource. If you are a one-person business chaotically trying to cover everything at all times you will never be able to separate out an area for allocation elsewhere.

As a really simple tool take a standard lever arch file and divide it into four subsections, one for each of the areas above-and then start compiling your systems manual.

As you identify and note each process that your business does you will create another sheet of paper to go into the relevant subset of your file. Of course, nowadays that file is likely to be online rather than a physical thing but always find it useful to imagine what that might look like.

The systems sheets

Let's look at what each sheet that systems file may look like.

Compare these two instructions:

a. Place an ad in the local paper.
b. Place an ad in the local paper that comes out on a Friday.
   Ads need to be placed by close of business on the Wednesday preceding publication.
   The ad can be submitted online but it's also worth calling the newspaper to see they have any special deals on advertising space at the moment.
   Call before 2.30 on any day as the lady (name of Sally) that takes down the adverts leaves then to pick up her children from school.
   Her direct line number is 0123 456 7890.
   The price of the ad tends to reduce the closer to the publication date and broadly costs £1 per column inch, or £5 for two-column inches plus a photo if you wait until the Wednesday to book.
   The paper will encourage you to book a block of adverts for the next month or so but we found it's

actually cheaper to book one week at a time as long as we can still get the discount.

Always try and get the advert placed on the right-hand page and as near to the edge of the page as possible and ask that our ad is not placed immediately next to any of our direct competitors.

Examples of adverts that we have used successfully in the past are filed with this note.

We can immediately see that approach A is a fairly limited instruction whereas approach B constitutes the beginning of the system. This series of instructions can now be printed off and filed in the sales and marketing part of our systems manual.

The list of instructions in approach B means that a total stranger could come and pick up the piece of paper, and the example adverts, and replicate that part of the business fairly easily.

In this case, even if the business owner leaves the country or falls under a bus the business is still secure and will run on regardless.

Systemisation

Ideally, then this is what a new business owner will do:

1. Wear the hat and allocate their time to each strand of the business accordingly.

2. Work out what tasks need to be done for each area and get on with them!

3. Once each task has been identified, create a systems

note of how to complete that task as demonstrated above with the advert.

4. You may find it easier to actually talk and record each task as you are doing it as that saves you time in writing up the notes later. My writing really took off when I purchased voice recognition software.

5. Then as the business expands, the notes expand. Using our simple example above it may be that in time we advertise in more than one newspaper and in different parts of the country. As each step in the expansion is made an additional note is created and placed in the file. In time booking of advertising space may become a full-time job for one person or team of people, but as the notes have expanded along with the business then they have the detail of the process and tasks that need to be done.

6. Eventually we could actually have one or more files just for booking of adverts itself and the systems file will eventually increase to a series of files or procedures. It is rumoured that McDonald's has the most extensive collection of systems files of any business and has a procedure even for how to wash lettuce.

It is easy to see how a system so detailed can create strength in the business because when systems are so clearly identified and noted there is a reducing need for management and sophistication of staff. The systems file itself will replace line management and intelligence such that a lower cost of staff can be employed.

7. Include a system note in each area for how to replace yourself. This may be actually recruiting someone or broadly preparing a specification for outsourcing. This

then provides the process or system for the second person to recruit the third, the third to recruit the fourth and so on. At this stage the system is self-perpetuating.

And at this stage, the system itself is saleable either as franchise manual or as part of the processes and assets of the business being sold off entirely.

Do these systems notes for each of the first three sections: sales and marketing, product and distribution and recording.

At Fielding Financial we run educational events and each event is completely systemised – even the placing of the pencils on the desk. Each event has its own systems notes and even has layout diagrams that go to the venues ahead of the team such that when the team arrive at the venue the room can often be laid out and ready to be 'dressed'.

There are two separate room layouts we use: one for introductory events and one for advanced events.

At this stage, all that YOU need to do is the important bit: the strategy, leadership and planning. And to do that you use the information from your system to help. As part of the record-keeping section, always record everything: number of leads needed to convert one into a paying customer, numbers of customers; pounds spent on advertising: calculate the cost of acquisition of a customer: average amount spent by the customer, number of times they repeat buy, how many customers cross-buy into other products, how much credit you get given by suppliers, how quickly your own cash comes in and so on.

That set of information is known as KPIs (Key Performance Indicators) and with decent KPIs, you can manage a business at a distance. Let's say you own a hat shop and you know that for every 100 people that come in the shop, 10 try on a hat, and one person buys a hat and that one person tends to buy at least one other product too (a hat pin or a hat box for instance). You now know that as long as you can drive 100 people into your shop – you will sell a hat. That's the KPI.

Now imagine you're on a beach in the Bahamas. You get your record keeper to text you the KPIs each Friday afternoon and one week the text comes in and says had 5000 people in the shop this week. You now KNOW even without being there that the shop must be running short of the stock of hats (and probably hatpins and hat boxes too) and you need to send in a re-order to the supplier and quick. You also know that you need more wrapping paper, till rolls etc than normal, it's a simple example but hopefully, you get the gist.

Let's imagine that weekly text comes into you on the beach and it says 0 customers in the shop this week; you can make decisions from that. There must be plenty of hats in stock so you can slow down your reorder time before you need order any hats from your supplier, you also know that you won't sell any more hats so your cash flow might suffer, and you can make a decision to hold back on supplier payments for instance.

Most of the business can be managed and directed from that series of KPIs and weekly text of information, so get to grips with that as early as possible.

These KPIs are what the record-keeping department is really about and even though I'm a Chartered Accountant by training, my view is that the statutory accounts or VAT return or whatever it may be – falls out of the record-keeping system as a by-product, and not as the priority here.

KPIs first, and accounts second! These topics are covered in more detail in the recording section.

Systems flow

As well as individual sheets of information about each specific process, also think about preparing systems flow charts on how the system works overall and what you do there is to start at a group of processes – let's say taking an order – and you map out the processes needed to get that order to completion. Traditionally there are divisions or decision points, so for instance, do we have the item in stock – if the answer is yes then one set of procedures are followed and if the answer is no then a different set of procedures are needed.

This helps you identify the flow of your business and where the decisions need to be made.

Here's an example:

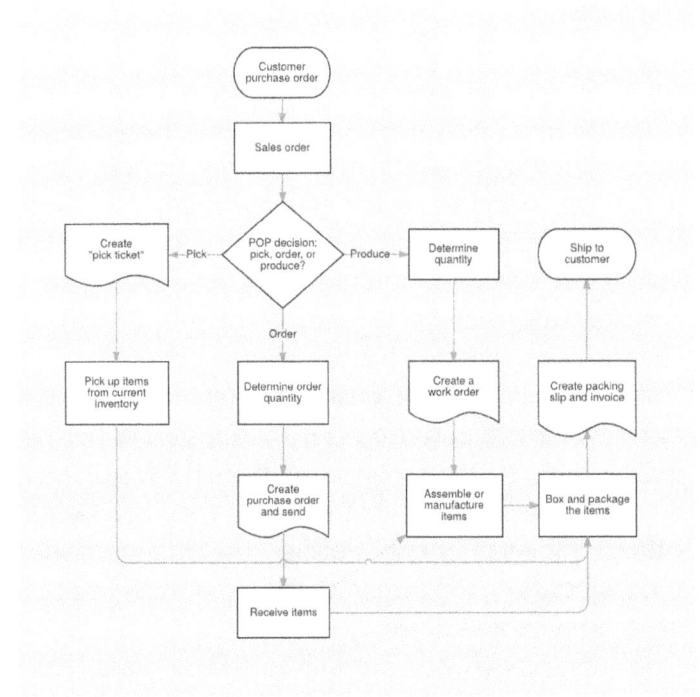

And then for each box on the flow chart, we would most likely have a systems or process sheet.

It may seem like complete overkill to do all this when you just get started because in the main all the information, decisions and processes are in your head but if your business is successful and it grows, this will be increasingly important and it's far easier to create the systems as you go rather than trying to remember and recreate later. Make the system itself part of the business, until the system can replicate the business without you.

If you hope that your business will eventually become successful enough to sell, then these systems manuals will be what any potential purchaser is looking for and the better the systems file the higher the price will be.

Processes

Hopefully, this will have given you some idea on how to create a systems note for your particular business or service and it's worth remembering to note down everything because even though many of these processes will be second nature to you personally that won't be the same for a third-party. As a check ask a friend or family member to read through the notes to see if they can understand what you are trying to do.

If we look back at the business pyramid, we can see that the ultimate purpose of any business is to be sold and it is these systems manuals that are the major asset in any business sale as that business then can be run without the initial business owner. That independence of business from the owner is what creates the biggest value in any business sale.

As I don't know what your individual business is, I can't create those systems notes for you here but the following is a series of tips, to help for ALL businesses.

And don't forget systems notes should contain examples, drawings, pictures and anything that helps to explain what's going on.

> *'Anything that is measured and watched, improves'-*
> **Bob Parsons, founder of GoDaddy**

If you are struggling with the concept here there will be a variety of reasons or excuses for your lack of enthusiasm but if you are struggling then could it be that you want the business to be dependent on you? I have seen many small business owners run themselves into the ground because the business was what gave them a sense of self-worth and to let it go or to ask for help was diminishing that.

Clearly to systemise the business is key to achieving greater wealth and this progression and here I am addressing taking a business and growing it organically from the bottom up, and up the five Tiers.

Most people, when they start a business don't get that and they think that the business is about THEM personally – and frankly, it isn't. Obviously, if all you want is to create a job then that's fine – but most businesses could be far more than that if only people could disconnect themselves from 'their baby'.

I am the Patron of the Chamber of Commerce in my area and I get to see so many businesses that are doomed to fail because of this fear of letting go and letting the business grow beyond the individual. What happens as a person goes up the Tiers with increasing systemisation, is that the business owner realises that they are no longer needed and they have, more or less, been replaced by a set of procedures manuals. And this is where we need to get back in touch with the Scales of Abundance and build up our belief in ourselves and what we do and be Ok with that because we are looking at a bigger wealth picture.

Maslow's hierarchy of need expresses a fairly sophisticated need 'to be needed' (the esteem needs) and what we are doing here is withdrawing that need, and many people just can't allow themselves NOT to be needed.

Maslow's Hierarchy of Needs

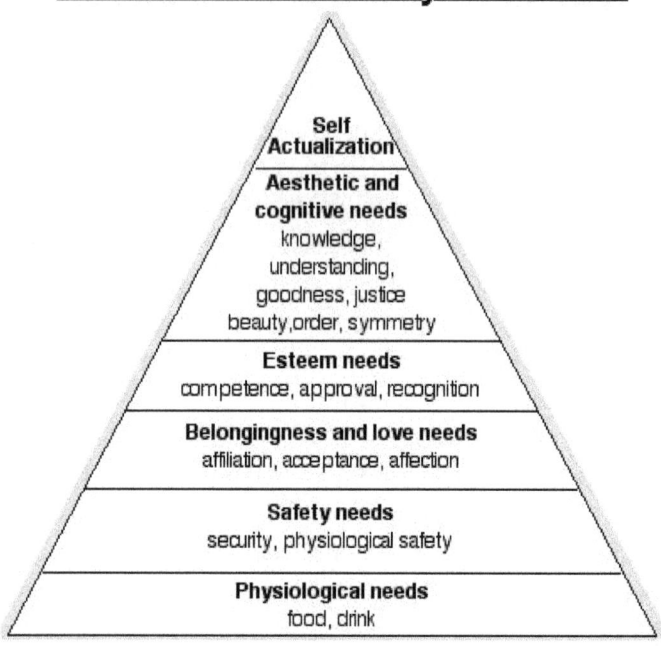

- **Self Actualization**
- **Aesthetic and cognitive needs**
  knowledge, understanding, goodness, justice, beauty, order, symmetry
- **Esteem needs**
  competence, approval, recognition
- **Belongingness and love needs**
  affiliation, acceptance, affection
- **Safety needs**
  security, physiological safety
- **Physiological needs**
  food, drink

They insist that they are the ONLY person who knows their business and how to do it. They become a processing bottleneck where every action and decision needs to go through them. They become paralysed with fear about making the wrong decision and the business grinds to a halt. I've seen it so many times, and sadly they are always wrong. Nobody is indispensable and the quicker we learn how irrelevant we are then the quicker our business grows.

I attend an exercise class and the teacher is good. She started with one type of class that I attended but she wanted to expand to other forms of exercise.

After class one day I chatted to her about business expansion as she had the makings of a great system: good customer information, the right music, the exercise steps in a logical methodology which would have been simple to write down and replicate. I suggested that she do that and get other teachers involved but she was adamant that she was the key to it all and without her nobody would come. I didn't have the heart to tell her that in all honesty all I was concentrating on was keeping up and listening to the instructions – and looking mainly at the back of her head – I couldn't have cared less who was shouting the instructions. Her expansion lasted a short while: she became frazzled and the quality dropped and become more erratic and uncertain and so people started to drop off and she's now back to Tier One again. She wanted to expand up to Tier Three but just couldn't detach herself from her business.

The Customer

The customer is at the heart and centre of any business (hence why the Customer is at the heart and centre of this book). Without the customer, there is no business, and of course, the customer is always right!

This creates some difficulty for smaller businesses. If you are an entrepreneur who loves their product or service, the fact that the customer might not like it as much is a challenge. It is vital therefore that every business owner quickly learns to apply the principle of:

TLC, or

Think **L**ike a **C**ustomer!

Some tips to help you here are:

1. Show your product to some customers and see if they buy it. If they do then you can start showing your product to more customers and then also start testing price points and product variants.

    IF they don't buy it then you need to find out why and it's vital to get feedback here. Is it price? Value? Poor quality? Lack of interest or need or desire? When you find out that then you need to find out if that is true for all customers – or at least another batch of them. If you show your product to a reasonable number of customers and they don't buy then you have to think again. Hopefully, you will get some good feedback and that may help with choosing a different product or direction. But at some stage, you may need to stop chasing that rainbow and accept that other people don't want your product as you hoped they might.

2. In the beginning, customers make a choice on what they see that's available so your product or service needs to stand up to scrutiny and comparison. Research what others do, what they offer and what they charge. You may need to go into the market at a lower price just to get yourself started.

    However, once the customer has bought from you a couple of times, they will start to develop product or brand loyalty and then the price points tend to be less important. BUT make sure you treat your customers well, you look after them and nurture them otherwise, eventually, they will go away.

That loyalty will eventually mean that you can cross-sell or upsell products to them.

3. The customer is always right and knows what they want. You have to accept that EVEN IF you're sure they are wrong and that you know better. The customer will tell you what they like and what they don't: they will tell you if they prefer the same but in blue, or with a longer handle, matching accessories or less packaging. Listen to them and test what they say against your standard product to see if their variant sells more than yours. You may be so in love with your product that you fail to see it objectively.

4. Your customer can become an important part of your marketing. They can give you feedback, referrals and testimonials. Make sure you include in your customer communication plans that you ask for these every now and then.

5. Listen to your customer and always show respect. Hear their concerns and in my experience, if you can correct a problem for a customer, they become more loyal than normal as they know you're listening and trust you to put it right.

6. Every now and then try and experience what your customer does. Put yourself in their shoes and go into your shop and try and buy something, flick through your web site and so on. Buy something and see how pleased you are with the service!

7. Recruit a mystery shopping service or a person who will experience your business and then tell it like it is!

Distribution and delivery

No customer will stay with you very long if your product is difficult to buy or to get access to. You have to find the quickest, easiest and most painless way to get the product from you to the customer. You may still have to offer alternatives as some customers prefer one method of delivery and some prefer others but any method you offer has to be slick.

Purchasing processes need to be painless and quick: for instance, if you're selling off the web can the customer get from the home page to the shopping basket and out quickly and intuitively. If you're selling in a shop are there enough tills or helpers?

Delivery times need to be short and exact. In the past I can remember when I would order my Christmas gifts from a catalogue in late November, allowing 21 or 28 days for delivery: nowadays a Christmas gift can be bought, delivered, wrapped, opened and thrown away – all in the space of 48 hours!

We live in an immediacy culture where people expect everything immediately. Build a despatch and delivery service and add the cost of that to the product cost – or pass that cost directly onto the customer, but that's not a popular thing as many suppliers now deliver for free.

And most importantly YOU need to do all the work and not the customer. It annoys me when I get put into an automated telephone queue and have to type in dates of birth, account numbers etc just to be asked them all again when I get through to an operator – how inconvenient and insulting to the customer is that because it's demonstrating that the supplier thinks their time is more important than yours as the customer.

Where you can prepopulate information you already know about a customer. A customer will know if you know their name and address and date of birth, so once you've collected that don't ask them again (other than for security checks) as a customer will just think you're inefficient.

The aim with distribution and delivery is to remove any potential barrier to the purchase and make that as painless as possible for the customer. If it's easy and they don't have to think about it, they will repeat buy.

Payment options

Ease of payment is vital. If it's complicated to pay or time-consuming then the customer's urge to buy will start to diminish. It's important that you take their money quickly and, in the method, they like to use, however difficult that may be for you.

My role is that if I, as a supplier, want to sell something

then it's my responsibility to do all the work. The customer always has the choice to go elsewhere.

Some customers still like cash, although this is decreasing, occasionally cheques, bank transfers, debit cards and credit cards. Customers like ease, swift, and mainly contactless, and if they can't buy in the swipe of a card then they're off!

Obviously, as a supplier, you want them to pay in the cheapest method for you as most debit and credit cards will charge you a fee and that can be substantial. Also bear in mind the time it takes for the money to get to you from the 'collector' as you could be waiting a few weeks for your hard-earned cash.

Build into your product price an average cash collection cost and review that from time to time. As you grow it's likely you will get better deals from the card companies so you should be able to reduce that cost over time.

B. The people (and their processes)

No business would be able to operate without people and in most businesses, they are the greatest asset. Consequently, they need looking after! Here are some of the areas of 'best practice' for having employees in your business.

> *'If you're good to your staff when things are going well, then they'll rally when times go bad.'* - **Mary Kay Ash**

Recruiting the right people!

Recruiting the right people into your business is essential. For teams small and large the right skills set and personality types are the key to a productive and happy workforce. One mistake hire can upset the delicate balance of any working environment.

Recruiting talent takes a combination of creativity and diligence. Today's technology now makes it easier than ever to publish your job postings to a broad audience—but to connect with the right candidates and drive excitement about the role and your company, you have to stand out.

What is a recruiting strategy?

A recruiting strategy is a plan of action to successfully identify, recruit and hire high-quality candidates. These are basic starting points that can help you attract the job seekers you are looking for. They range from basic methods, like posting on job boards, to more advanced methodologies, such as engaging a recruitment agency or creating a referral program.

> *'The secret to successful hiring is this: look for the people who want to change the world.'* - **Marc Benioff, Salesforce CEO**

1. Treat candidates like customers

Whether it's a phone screening or an in-person interview, a candidate's first impression of your company is critical. It's important you make them feel you're as excited about getting to know them as they are about being considered for the role. One of the best recruiting techniques is to treat interviewees the same way you treat your customers.

- **Be respectful of their time.** Whether it's a phone call, video conference or in-person meeting, always be sure to show up on time. If you're running late, let the candidate know as far in advance as possible.
- **Be hospitable.** When a candidate arrives for an in-person interview, ask if they'd like something to drink and show them where to find the restrooms. Make them feel as welcome and comfortable as possible.
- **Make yourself available.** Provide candidates with your contact information so they're able to reach out with questions and concerns throughout the process.

2. Use social media

Social media is a fantastic recruiting tool. Social recruiting allows you to share job postings with your entire network and encourages a two-way conversation. Even if the people you reach aren't interested in the role for which you're hiring, it's likely they may know someone who is a good fit. Also, by sharing photos and videos from company events or day-to-day office life, you give potential applicants a glimpse into your company culture
.

3. Create compelling job descriptions

Writing an attention-grabbing and thorough job description is crucial to engaging with qualified candidates.

Here are a few tips to consider:
- **Make titles as specific as possible.** The more accurate your title, the more effective you will be in piquing the interest of the most qualified and interested job seekers.
- **Open with a captivating summary.** Provide an overview that gets job seekers excited about the role and the company.
- **Include the essentials.** Include core responsibilities, hard and soft skills, day-to-day activities and explain how the position fits into the organisation.
- **Keep descriptions concise.** Job descriptions between 700 and 2,000 characters receive up to 30% more applications according to Indeed Data.*

4. Make use of online recruitment sites

There are thousands of jobs posted online every day, so job listing visibility can diminish over time. Paid listings are prominently displayed at the top and bottom of any relevant search results pages, and their placement won't fall with time like free job listings—which results in more high-quality applicants. So, when you start a recruitment drive it is worth agreeing and ring-fencing a small budget to help you find the right candidate

5. CV's

So, you have run a great recruitment campaign and you have been inundated with CV's. Where do you start? Below are some top tips for spotting great candidates:

1. **Communications skills**
   This is one of the most valued personal skills a candidate can have. You are looking for interesting, well written and easy to read CV's. It should be well put together and clear, thereby showing they have excellent written as well oral skills.

2. **CV layout**
   You want to be able to see employment history easily and clearly, so look out for neat CV's with easy to find sections with clear headings and bullet points to emphasise areas of expertise.

3. **Any relevant experience**
   Providing evidence of experiences that are related to the competencies required. Has the applicant showcased those skill sets most relevant to the job?

4. **Related academic qualifications**
   Has the candidate listed the educational

achievements that are related to a vacancy?

5. **Market or product knowledge**
   Does the CV Showcase an in-depth experience of how the industry operates or of a specific product or service that you as a business owner supplies. Knowledge of competitors is also a plus.

6. **Problem solving capabilities**
   Does your applicant give examples of how they resolved or found solutions to difficult scenarios? Applicants should show that they are achievers, who have the drive to meet goals.

7. **Planning and organisational skills**
   Does this applicant have the ability to gather information, analyse results, monitor performance and plan ahead.

8. **Being specific**
   For instance, do they mention that they increased sales of product x by 50% during a 6-month period, or saved the company £4k by changing suppliers for office stationery?

9. **Being human!**
   This person needs to fit within your company. Do they have hobbies and interests which would help them gel with the existing team? The human element of a CV helps showcase the type of person they are and how they could potentially fit with other employees. This element also gives you something to break the ice with if they get to an interview!

The interview

So, you have selected your 4 or 5 top candidates for the job. Next is the interview.

Interviews can be daunting for employers and potential employees alike.

From the outset, you need to determine if you are going to conduct a formal or an informal interview.

Informal Interview

It's easy to see why many candidates and employers prefer informal interviews. They often take place outside of the office and are generally a lot less stressful than a full-on face to face meeting. Because of this, candidates usually feel a lot more relaxed and confident when it comes to this type of interview, but it's important to remember that this is still part of the selection process. Whatever is said during these informal conversations will still have an impact on whether or not you wish to ask them back for a more formal interview.

An informal interview allows you the employer to get a more natural feel for a candidate's personality type and whether they would or wouldn't work well within the existing team structure.

Formal Interview

A more formal interview is typically carried out in a more formal office setting. Normally an employer would be accompanied by a note-taker or HR manager.
On average the interview would last for about an hour and could follow a more structured approach:

1. An employer takes a little time to talk about the company, its mission and its goals.

2. The candidate would be asked to recap their career to date.

3. There would then be a series of competency-based questions relevant to the job role. For example, "Can you tell me about a time you had to deal with a customer complaint?" or "Can you tell me of a time when a decision had been made which you felt was wrong - how did you manage that situation?".

4. Competency questions should be relevant to the role on offer. They are a superb way of understanding how people react in various situations.

5. It may also be appropriate to have given the applicant an exercise to complete ahead of the interview or to prepare to make a presentation. We use this a lot when we recruit for marketing team members – it's important that in marketing you can see flare and creativity from the outset.

6. The competency part of the interview can be quite formal and can often leave the candidate a little exhausted. Most employers will be looking for certain answers and as such may probe in-depth. It is therefore always good practise to end the interview asking about hobbies and interests outside of work. It is also important to tell the candidate when they may expect to hear about the next stage or receive an outcome and stick to that date or at least inform them if the date changes – there is nothing worse than not knowing if you have been successful.

It is also good practise to offer feedback to candidates who weren't successful. Do take care though not to discriminate candidates due to age, gender, ethnicity or disability as this is against the law.

Offer up helpful tips which may assist them with their next interview.

> *'Nothing we do is more important than hiring people. At the end of the day, you bet on people, not strategies'-*
> **Lawrence Bossidy**

Introduction to HR

As a business owner, your people are your biggest asset. You will hope that your employees have a long and rewarding career within your business and for that reason, it is important for both the employee and employer that you have clear Employment Policies and Procedures in place. These policies and procedures normally take the form of a colleague handbook or HR policy booklet.

The HR policy document should cover the Company's policies and procedures. As such they are not taken as contractual clauses but are regarded as the Company's best practice and are designed to ensure safety, efficiency, transparency and compliance with the Company's legal obligations. Whilst they do not have a contractual effect a breach of a policy could lead to disciplinary action.

For many companies, they may operate for a good number of years with a loyal and trustworthy team of people. Good and kind management often results in excellent loyalty and productivity but even the best business can sometimes find themselves with an HR issue they could not foresee.

It is therefore vital for any business that they protect themselves and their employees with clear and detailed HR policies.

Why should you have an HR Policy in place?

There are certain HR policies all UK businesses are required to have in place by law because they are seen as vital to the day to day running of any business:

Health & Safety

Under the Health and Safety at Work 1974 act, if you employ 5 or more employees you must have a written general Health & Safety policy.

The importance of health and safety in the workplace simply cannot be underestimated. As well as being the law, it is part and parcel of being a good employer to make sure your staff aren't at risk of any injury as a result of the work they do for you.

It's not just for your staff that health and safety rules are important, it's also there to protect any visitors, customers, sub-contractors and the general public who may work for you, do business with you or come into contact with your organisation in any way.

Poor health and safety can lead to illness, injury and even death - you can be prosecuted for breaching health and safety regulations which can lead to fines, imprisonment and the loss of your business altogether. Now that may seem extreme but it is imperative that you have clear policies and guidelines in place to protect all parties including yourself!

Employee Rights

The majority of people who will work for you will be classed as employees. You're classed as an employee if you're working under a contract of employment.

- *Rights of employees*

As an employer, you are obliged by law to deduct Income Tax and National Insurance contributions from your employees' salary or wages before paying them. Employees are also entitled to all minimum legal employment rights including:
- statutory sick pay
- maternity, adoption and paternity leave and pay
- the right not to be unfairly dismissed

- legal redundancy pay
- all the rights that are given to 'workers' (below)

Some of these rights require a minimum length of continuous employment before an employee qualifies for them. An employment contract may state how long this qualification period is.

- *A Worker*

A worker is any individual who works for you the employer, whether under a contract of employment, or any other contract where an individual undertakes to do personally any work or services for you or your company.

Workers are entitled to core employment rights and protections. The following groups of people are likely to be workers but not employees:
- most agency workers
- short term casual workers
- some freelancers,

Providing any other qualifying conditions are met, all workers have rights to:
- the National Minimum Wage
- rest breaks, paid holiday and limits on night work
- protection against unauthorised deductions from pay
- maternity, paternity and adoption pay (but not leave)
- protection against less favourable treatment if they make a disclosure in the public interest (often called 'whistleblowing')
- not be discriminated against unlawfully
- Working time limits (the 48-hour week)

Employees

Under the Employment Rights Act, 1996 employers are required to give all employees a written statement of their Employment Terms & Conditions, which includes rules and procedures for dealing with grievances and disciplinary issues.

Although not statutory you would expect a business to have policies for the following areas:

- Data Protection
- Induction Policy and Procedure
- Recruitment and selection policy and procedure
- Internal communications
- Filming in the office
- Dress code
- Holidays
- Working time
- Part-time working
- Sickness absence
- Stress management
- Special and Compassionate leave
- Time off to deal with domestic emergencies
- Time off for public duties
- Time off for dependents
- Time off for medical or dental appointments
- Right to request time off for training
- Training payment policy
- Maternity
- Adoption leave
- Paternity leave
- Shared parental leave
- Resignation

- References
- Disciplinary procedure
- Capability procedure
- Policy to review performance
- Performance review procedure
- Capability sickness absence
- Capability illness and disability
- Grievance
- Expenses
- Business travel
- Personal telephone calls
- Mobile phone use
- Using tablets/computers during working hours
- Email and internet use
- Social media
- Equal opportunities
- Equal pay
- Equality and diversity
- Anti-harassment and bullying
- Managing personal relationships at work
- Health and safety at work
- Lone working
- Homeworking
- Behaviour at work-related social events
- Alcohol and drugs
- Smoke-free
- Severe weather
- Corporate gifts and hospitality
- Anti-bribery
- Whistleblowing
- Bonus Policy
- Pay Policy
- GDPR policies and SAR policies and procedures

Now that's quite some list – but do not fret.

We have created a template for you to download at www.businessforwealth.com. You can take this template and personalise it to your business needs.

Advantages of having a policy in place

To be a successful business owner you should have prepared and updated good personnel management policies and in doing so there are several important ways in which they contribute to the success of any business enterprises. Many observers have pointed out that even the best policies will falter if the business owners or managers who are charged with administering those policies are careless or incompetent in doing so. But for those businesses that are able to administer their HR policies in an intelligent and consistent manner, benefits can be seen in several areas:

Curbing litigation. As a business owner, you can do a lot to cut off legal threats from disgruntled current or ex-employees simply by creating—and applying—a fair and comprehensive set of personnel policies. Clear HR policies protect all parties and clears up any ambiguity.

Communication with employees. A good, written human resource policy manual can be an enormously effective tool in disseminating employer expectations regarding worker performance and behaviour. It leaves no grey areas and whilst an employer may wish to be more generous with elements like maternity leave etc a clear policy delivers transparency to the workplace.

Communication with managers and supervisors. Formal policies can be helpful to managers and other supervisory personnel faced with hiring, promotion, and reward decisions concerning people who work under them.

Time Savings. Prudent and comprehensive human resource management policies can save companies significant amounts of management time that can then be spent on other business activities, such as new product development, competitive analysis, marketing campaigns, etc

When you need to make a change to your HR policy

Once you have a clear set of HR policies businesses typically have to make revisions on an annual basis, as the company grows and as the regulatory and business environments in which it operates evolve. When confronted with the challenge of updating HR policies, however, it is important for small businesses to proceed cautiously. For example, if an employee asks the owner of a small business if he might work from his home one day a week, the owner may view the request as a reasonable, relatively innocuous one. But even minor variations in personnel policy can have repercussions that extend far beyond the initially visible parameters of the request. If the employee is granted permission to work from home one day a week, will other employees ask for the same benefit?

Does the employee expect the business to foot the bill for any aspect of the working from home? Do customers rely on the employee (or employees) to be in the office five days a week – are they customer-facing? Do other employees need that worker to be in the office to answer questions? Is the nature of the employee's workload such that he can take meaningful work home?

As business owners, we need to recognise that changes in HR policy have the potential to impact, in one way or another, every person in the company, *including* the owner. Proposed changes should be examined carefully and in consultation with others within the business who may recognise potential pitfalls that other managers, or the business owner himself, might not detect. Once a change in policy is made, it should be disseminated widely and effectively so that all employees are aware.

Performance management

The aim of any performance management tool is to improve the capability of employees at work, hence making them work more effectively. Carried out correctly, as well-executed performance management will act as a form of motivator and will help the employees grow and develop over time. However, effective performance management is also used to address areas for development or underperformance. It is hoped that this can be achieved without any disciplinary action – but it is accepted that, in certain cases, this will be necessary as a final resort.

The key blocks to any performance management structure are:

1. Assessment of capability

The assessment of capability is an ongoing process within the organisation. It starts at the stage of recruitment when the employee is assessed as being capable of doing the job. It is likely that the employee will need additional training when first employed – and this will be addressed during the induction process.

On an on-going basis, capability is assessed through the supervision and appraisal process. If any capability difficulties are addressed during this process the manager conducting the supervision and appraisal and the employee are required to draw up an action plan together to address the issue.

2. Induction

All new employees should attend an appropriate induction. The details of the induction process will form part of your own individual HR policy document as they differ from company to company but as a rule of thumb new recruits should be clear on a company's strategy, mission and values. They must also be aware of all relevant H&S and GDPR implications.

It is important, however, that any learning and development interventions which address capability are identified and addressed during the induction process.

3. Responsibilities of the employee

- Your employee is required to work effectively and to perform to the highest standard achievable.
- If the employee is struggling in any area of his/her work, that employee should speak to the manager and ask for assistance. Admitting the need for assistance is not seen as a weakness.
- The employee is responsible for working with the manager during supervisions to agree with an appropriate way to address any capability difficulties.
- The employee is responsible for attending any learning and development activities that are planned to enhance his/her performance at work.
- The employee is also responsible for identifying any learning and development activities which might enhance work performance.
- The employee must be aware that the manager has a limited budget for learning and development events, and hence it might not always be possible to give permission to pursue a learning and development activity.

4. Responsibilities of the manager

- You or your appointed manager are responsible for meeting with all new starters and identifying any training or other interventions that are required to help the new starter work effectively within the team.
- You or your appointed manager are responsible for carrying out appraisals and supervisions with all his/her team, in accordance with the appraisals policy. All

appraisals should be completed in a timely manner.
- If any capability issues are identified during the appraisal and supervisions process the manager is responsible for working with the employee to draw up an appropriate action plan to address the issue(s) that have been identified.
- You or your appointed manager are responsible for setting appropriate targets for the employee to achieve and for monitoring the progress of any employee who is working in accordance with an action plan, and identifying and addressing any issues that arise which mean the targets within that plan are not being met.

5. Succession planning

The purpose of succession planning is to identify employees who show a potential capability for promotion in the future. If an employee is placed on a succession plan the department manager, in conjunction with senior management, should identify what additional abilities the employee will need to be capable in the more senior role in the future.

To achieve those additional abilities the employee might need:
- To attend appropriate training courses
- Coaching or mentoring
- Exposure to work in other departments
- Opportunities to deputise for their manager
- Other opportunities

You or your appointed manager should work with the employee to design a programme of activities which allow the employee to develop the required capabilities.

In doing this, it is important that no promises are made of certain promotion unless they can be guaranteed.

6. Promotion

If an employee is promoted at work, then the new manager of that employee should meet with the employee to discuss any additional training or other learning and development that is required to ensure the capability of the employee in the new role.

The organisation is responsible for the careful consideration of all promotions, and should not promote employees unless they have the necessary abilities.

7. Monitoring of capability issues

You or your appointed manager are responsible for monitoring the performance of employees. If the employee is not achieving the agreed targets after interventions have taken place, a further meeting will take place between the employee and the manager.

In summary *it is essential for any business that key elements like transparent recruitment processes, clear HR polices and well-managed performance management processes are in place and well documented BUT it is also important that you keep your team of employees motivated and happy.*

Little gestures go a long way like a team text on a Friday night to say "thank you", or a surprise "Jacket potato Thursday" (always a hit in our office) or making the effort to bake some cakes–what office doesn't like cake!

Employees are the lifeblood of any business, big or small, and they should be valued and appreciated. The formal HR elements should run alongside friendly, caring management–done correctly you will create a loyal and hardworking team of advocates who enjoy their job and who always put the customer first because they care about the company and care about you!

Erzsebet Kohut: Story

Before I share my story, let me give you a short introduction on what I do.

Almost 15 years ago, my business partner and I opened a day nursery. https://www.seedlingsdaynursery.com/

We cater for local demand in our area (Forest Hill, London) for working families whose children are 0-4 years. We have always worked with full capacity and currently have 74 families on roll. We are open all year around, Monday to Friday, 8am-6pm. The nursery employs 20 staff members, some of whom are with us for a long period of time.

We soon learnt that the key to running a successful nursery is employing the right staff who are dedicated, want to maintain regular work and are happy to learn. The equation is very simple.

Happy staff =happy children=happy parents

I guess it is the same in the property business, where I will have to find the right power team, treat them well and grow together. Sounds simple.

However, in recent years things changed for us working in the nursery world. The market became a 100% 'candidate led" which means that there are more desperate settings wanting to attract good workforce, but only a few suitable candidates are available. It's almost like candidates dictate how much they want to earn and what conditions they want to work under. And who can offer more pay, more holiday entitlement and flexible work, will win the candidate.

This is a problem. We have to have a high expectation of staff, not only because we are Ofsted rated outstanding but we are caring for other people's children who pay a lot of money to access our services.

So, this is how we found ourselves recruiting constantly for the past 2 years. This is due to maternity leaves, colleagues moving out of the area, wanting a career change and 2 of them are on long-term sick leave.

So why is the change in recent years? It is a lot to do with people not wanting to work 40 hours a week anymore. Some can't because they might have family commitments or simply by working, they lose out on their benefit entitlements. It is no longer worth it for them to work and earn almost the same amount as if they stayed on benefits. I always wondered when will the government realise that it is not encouraging for people to engage in employment. We have had decent staff leaving us before for this reason.

Also, recruitment agencies (http://www.networkrs.co.uk/about-us/) started to struggle to recruit staff as well. Therefore, they introduced new initiatives to attract candidates into temporary work- package deals that are difficult to beat. They are offered flexible working hours, holiday pay and a decent hourly rate.

But even then, they are struggling to find new recruits. When rarely they have someone, they are charging us around £2000-£3000, but there is no guarantee the staff will stay on. We have had someone leaving after 4 weeks, deciding that staying in the UK was no longer an option for her.

Although I can see why the agency deal is appealing to many, we have had no joy in recruiting from them.

In our business continuity remains crucial so that children's routines are not interrupted, so we really have to find the right permanent workforce for the smooth running of our operation.

So, we started thinking outside the box, how can we make our job vacancy more attractive. During the recruitment process we met people who although were qualified but lacked enthusiasm, willingness and simply looked sour in themselves.

We had a candidate on a trial day from an agency who told us she is 'popping out to the pharmacy' and never returned. Nor the agency or we heard from this lady again.

And these are just a few examples.

You might be wondering if we are a decent company to work for. Well, I can confirm that we really look after our staff. We care about each one of them and try to be flexible with family commitments and offer competitive wages, etc.

It seems like simply this is the current era as all the other nurseries and agencies are in the same situation.

Alongside this, nurseries had to up their standards due to new and higher expectations from the government. This poses us constant challenges as we need to balance out the following:
- Keeping standards high and meeting new statutory requirements
- Keeping our current team happy to make sure they stay
- Trying to recruit new staff to balance out numbers and fill in for those on long-term sick leave

So, after all the hopeless interviews of unhappy people ☹ we decided to employ and train **unqualified** staff who are willing to learn, love children, enthusiastic and fun to have around.

We recently appointed 3 of these staff and they are wonderful additions to our team! They come from all sorts of backgrounds but are very willing, and by simply applying common sense they became very helpful to us. It is still within the legal expectations, as we have plenty of qualified staff around.

So, what we have learnt from this:
- Qualification doesn't guarantee dedication
- Experience and common sense are preferred over qualification
- Qualification and the amount of knowledge will depend on the training provider and the individual

Recruitment remains a constant battle for us and others in the nursery business. We are trying our utmost best to carry on providing an outstanding and fun environment for our children. And who knows? Maybe, like our recent recruits, this is the way forward, to offer permanent vacancies to those who want to learn and come with little or no experience or qualification. Willingness and common sense are key.

REPORTING

Introduction

I have to start this section by admitting that I'm not a huge fan of reporting.

This may be a strange thing for a chartered accountant to say, but although I have been both a Finance Director and a Compliance Officer, I do not relish form filling. Obviously, there are regulatory and legal requirements for any business to fulfil, but the systems we introduce to comply with all that can be far better used to provide the fundamental data needed for any business to grow and prosper.

Therefore, I want to split this section into two component parts:
- The standard reporting requirements. This will include all the taxation requirements, plus any company secretarial reporting that is needed if your business is structured as a company, plus a brief nod to other regulatory requirements that you may need. In the main, this information is retrospective and historic.
- The information and data required to monitor and manage any business. These are the management information systems (MIS) and the key performance indicators (KPIs). In the main, this information is created for future requirements.

Although the legal and formal reporting requirements must be done, any business owner should be building reporting systems that monitor the lifeblood of their business. The necessary formal reporting should purely be a by-product of the management information system built to control and provide information to the owner of the business.

There are many computers and Internet-based systems that will do most of the formal reporting very easily for all but the largest or unusual of organisations. The Internet will give you a good guide here, but simplicity is the key. No business owner wants to spend any of their precious resources on constant recording and reporting of facts and figures for a variety of government departments.

Ideally, any system used should be adaptable enough to provide the more important and fundamental business data needed, however that may not always be possible but it is always important to keep that end in mind.

I'm grateful to Debbie Franklin for providing an overview plus some detail of the formal and legal reporting requirements needed for any business, and that information is covered in Part Two of this session.

Part One of this session will cover the management information systems and KPIs and how to create and monitor those pieces of data.

Part One: MIS and KPIs

Management Information Systems (MIS)

Firstly, a management information system is any procedure that business has to collect data. This may be as simple as a human being pressing a clicker to count footfall every time a customer comes into the shop, all the way up to incredibly sophisticated computerised systems monitoring every detail and every movement of every part of the business.

It is important for any small business and every potential business owner to think about management information systems early on. In the early days many entrepreneurs are bound up in the emotion of their potential business. The creation of management information systems and KPIs gives the business owner the necessary feedback to see objectively what the business is doing and where it is going. Most small business owners love their business and their product and make decisions based partly on emotion, intuition and instinct. Whilst this is a great set of attributes to have, it is fundamental that the business owner also gets external and independent information to help with clearer judgement. MIS provides that.

Obviously, MIS can become incredibly complicated when the business is larger but can be quite simple and straightforward for the smaller organisation. Start with something simple and allow your MIS to grow and develop alongside the business overall.

Key Performance Indicators (KPIs)

KPIs are the parts of your MIS that you want to measure and there are some general KPIs that every business will want to monitor and then there are those that are more specific to your particular product or marketplace. For instance, every business needs to know how much cash they have and how much profit they are making. These figures should fall easily out of any reporting system that you install. However, the amount of material wasted in saying a dressmaking operation is a very specific KPI needed only for that industry.

It is not always so obvious as to what KPIs a business needs, and you need to be careful that you are not monitoring the wrong thing. The KPIs are the information on which most business decisions are made, so it is important to get these rights.

When considering what KPIs to monitor always put yourself in the position of being completely distant, hands off and passive in your business. If you spent your life on a beach in Barbados, what would you need to know each week to keep your finger on the pulse and to make the relevant business decisions.

Let's take a business as simple as a hat shop. You have a MIS that collects three pieces of information: the number of customers who come into the hat shop: the number of customers who try on a hat and finally the number of customers that buy a hat. The simplicity, let's say for every 10 customers that into the shop, three try on a hat and one finally purchases a hat.

From your beachside idyll all you need to know is that 10 customers came into the shop that day for you to know that your business is on track. If you receive this information by text from your shop manager, for instance, then you can relax. If, however, you receive a text to say that only five customers came into the shop then you have decisions to make. Do you need to reduce the number of hats that you order from your supplier? If you only had five customers, then there is a good chance you won't be selling any hats today. From this basic piece of information, you may be having to make decisions about the number of shop assistants you need: the number of hat boxes you need for packaging and the amount of stock you are holding.

Conversely, if you receive a text from your shop

manager that 20 customers came into the shop today you immediately know you need to order more stock from your supplier because it's likely that you are going to be selling double the number of hats. In addition, you may need to purchase more packaging and ramp up any other ancillary resource.

Clearly this is a very simple and naïve example and no decision should be made on information so basic or short-term, but it should give you some idea of what information you may need and how that information can be used.

The aim of any MIS and KPIs collected is to give you an independent error-free methodology of making judgements and decisions about your business today and in the future.

Finally, and before we leap into a long list of potential KPIs, it is important that you concentrate on only a few. If you are having to produce, monitor or control a huge long list of KPIs, then you have created a problem. Most businesses should have only a handful of real crunch points that need your attention.

Each business requires different KPIs and yours may be very specific. Concentrate on finding what they are. Let's now start looking at a selection of KPIs in different parts of the business, and from that you should then be able to create your own particular set.

Key Performance Indicators

It is true that most businesses will require some KPIs on every section of their business, but again this can become unwieldy. In order of priority, my recommendation is that you start with sales and cash as without those your business is finished. Thereafter you may want KPIs for your marketing team, your HR Department and certainly for most processing areas. Once you have worked out what it is, you need to measure, then of course you need to implement the MIS to collect the relevant data.

Cash flow

Fundamentally cash needs to be flowing into your business and in the early days you will probably know to the cent or penny what cash you have and how much you need.

1. The baseline KPI is the amount of cash that you need in order to cover the overheads and pay the bills even if you do not sell anything! This is often a tough number to accept and consequently many small business owners underestimate this figure, particularly as these costs tend to be covered out of the owner's pocket in the early days.

    Nonetheless, it is vital that you know what you are letting yourself in for realistically and depending on the type of business that you have started it would be sensible to make sure that you have approximately 3 to 6 months money available to cover this overhead and dead costs.

2. Then we add to that baseline KPI the amount of money needed to run the business in a small way. The costs that we will incur here are the costs of purchasing or creating any stock to sell, plus any other marginal costs needed to get that product into

the hands of a paying customer. This could include transportation and packaging costs, for instance. These are generally known as the marginal costs of sale as they are the extra amount of money we need to pay per item of product or service.

3. And then we scale up! It is useful to have a KPI measure for each level of your potential business bearing in mind that there are economies of scale as you get larger but there will also be tipping points where you have to employ say one extra person who may be underutilised at first.

Once you have got the measure on your cash outflows and your cost base, you can start adding some cash inflows, but please always be prudent here.

In essence, cash is King - and Queen of any business! Make sure you have it!

You also have to consider timing. Your supplier may need paying in 30 days and your customer may pay on day one, which means you are always ahead of the game but nonetheless the supplier will still need paying later on. There are some businesses where the reverse happens and although your supplier insists on being paid in 30 days, your customer refuses to part with any cash for a couple of months and again you need to be able to cover that. You do also need some contingency here because there could be times when both your customer and your supplier changes their normal payment pattern because of specific things happening in their business and not yours.

It is unfortunate that particularly small businesses often get manipulated by larger suppliers and customers who have more clout, and there has been many a small business gone under because they are providing a product or service to a large organisation who dictate their own payment terms.

However, in the main most small businesses will soon get into a reasonable cash flow and will know that a certain amount of money needs to go out every month but, all being well, a certain amount of money also comes in. Identify how much money needs to come in on a regular basis in order to cover all overhead, fixed and marginal costs plus making sure there is enough also to pay yourself.

When creating MIS for your cash flow make sure that your system reports peaks and troughs because it is unlikely that your cash flow will be exactly the same each month and any excess in one-month should be placed to one side to manage the shortfall in another.

Any bank manager or fund provider will want to see a detailed cash flow forecast from you which covers at least the next 12 months and then a summary cash flow for maybe a couple of years thereafter. Although you may not be requiring an overdraft or loan facility from an external source, you should still calculate these cash flows in order to provide the necessary discipline and knowledge of the business for yourself.

Sales and Profit

The next KPI to measure is sales – and by that I mean genuine external, proper sales – not discounted sales to your aunt!

To record this, just add up the full sales price of anything sold. That should be easy as long as you're recording the number of units sold and the price.

Then you can calculate your profit, which tends to come in two versions:
- Gross profit, and
- Net profit

When you're just starting out, or if your business is fairly simple, there may not be much, if any, difference between these two figures, but broadly the gross profit is the sales less the cost of the sale, and that's usually the cost price of the product or service that you pay to your supplier. The difference between your cost and the price you sell is the gross margin, or gross profit

Net Profit

Then from that gross profit you deduct all your other costs – and I mean all – to get to your genuine net profit or earnings for you in the business. As a very rough rule of thumb, I suggest you set a target for this net profit to be approximately 10%. If you want to be more sophisticated than that as a measure, then go onto a government statistics website like the Office for National Statistics in the UK and they will have average profitability measures for most industries or markets. You can then compare yourself and your profitability to others in the same sector.

Here's an example for a simple, retail business:

Sales	£50,000
Cost of sales:	£15,000
Gross Profit	**£35,000**
Less:	
Overheads: Rents & Rates	£7,500
Wages	£15,000
Printing and stationery items	£2,500
Other	£2,500
Net profit	**£7,500**

The gross profit percentage here is 70% and the net profit percentage is 15%.

The reason it is important to record and review both the gross profit percentage and the net profit is that it's fairly easy to 'buy' sales and by that, I mean offering sufficiently large discounts on the sales price just to get a sale – but of course that takes all the profit.

In the case of the simple example above, if we assume the sales are of 10,000 units at £5 each with a cost of £1.5 each, we could think that we have plenty of margin to play with but if we discount the sales price by £1 to £4 then our gross profit becomes £25,000 and our net profit becomes a loss of £2,500.

NEVER target your sales force with just a sales unit sold figure.

> **Basic Three KPIs**
>
> Our first three KPIs for any – and all businesses then are:
> Cash
> Sales
> Profit (both gross and net) %

Thereafter KPIs tend to be more business or industry specific but these are some suggestions in broad categories for you to consider as right for you.

Sales and Profit: Second Tier

Once we have those headline KPIs in place, we can then analyse a little further. Here are some possible KPIs to consider:

Sales and Customers

1. Number of existing and new customers. This will give you some idea of expansion or potential growth.

2. Average customer spend. At the basic level this measures the amount or number of products your customer is buying but this is also relevant if your customer has choices and options to buy a variety of products and this KPI measures your ability to upsell and cross sell from the first product purchased into the full range. If a customer comes into your shop and buys a book, for example, do you also sell them a diary, some pencils, and get them to visit your coffee shop! If you know that the average price of a

book is say £/$10 but the average customer spend is £/$15 that gives you a measure of the 'extra' sale, and from that target the business to increase the average customer spend over time.

As usual with sales, be careful here to not sacrifice profit for sales as increasing customer average spend may take them away from your most profitable product or service. Use both KPIs to get the balance you want.

3. Lifetime value of a customer. If your product or service has a facility for a customer to repeat buy (and most of them do), how successful are you in getting the customer to come back and buy again, repeatedly? This measures partly the customer care (a customer won't come back again if they are dissatisfied) but also the efficiency of presenting the customer with the repeat experience appropriately: how easily can you make that experience?

In addition, with this one, it may be the measure of how long you can keep the customer interested with, say a subscription product where they pay monthly. If they start to 'drop off' after say month 7, can you identify why that is and what can you do to extend that to 8 months or 9 and so on.

4. As well as the sales figures, measure the growth in sales. What do you want that growth to be? This is an ideal targeting exercise.

5. Timings: Depending on the type of business you have, you may need to measure processes, such as production times, delivery times, time for fulfilment of orders and so on. We live in an immediacy culture

nowadays where customers want their product NOW. If you can't do that, then your customer will go to someone who can.

6. Customer satisfaction: feedback and promoter scores. The better your feedback, the better your business and you need to monitor and measure that actively. Due to the virtual world, good feedback is vital, so keep your eye on it: monitor google reviews and any ratings systems for your product. Don't ignore bad reviews: follow up and resolve where possible and show the virtual world you take notice.

Marketing and Sales Measures

In this group we can look at all KPIs including social media which is very wide ranging and you will have to find your own 'crunch' points but some examples are:

1. Cost per lead. This is a vital KPI. How much are you paying to get each lead you need? This may be old-fashioned media advertising, or TV or blogs or search engine based, or possibly all the above. Wherever the leads come from, you need to measure how much each lead costs you, and that then drives your marketing spend or budget. To calculate this, simply take the marketing spend already incurred and divide it by the number of leads you generated with that money.

2. Lead conversion. Then calculate how many sales you got from those leads. Are you converting 1 in a 100 or 1 in 10? There's a huge difference and that conversion rate needs to be as low as possible.

3. Acquisition cost per customer. This is one of my favourite KPIs as it measures the cost of getting each individual customer, which when compared to the average sale per customer should give you a very clear indication of potential profitability and the strength of your business.

   Calculate this by looking at the most recent events: how many new customers did you gain in that period and how much did you spend to get them: include all marketing costs and any support costs.

Web sites

1. Monthly or daily traffic: how many people do you need on your website each day to create the orders or interaction you need?

2. Heat maps: websites can be monitored now to see where the customer is looking and clicking: are your customers looking at the right pages? What new fashions or protocols are there in the wider world that changes how your customer looks at a website. You need to keep your web site current and immediate and focused on where you want the customer to go.

3. How many 'clicks' to purchase? How quickly can you get the customer to the shopping cart and buying? The fewer the better.

4. Leads to purchase ratios. How many leads do you have to drive to your website before a sale is made?

This measures the efficiency of the website and also maximises the profitability of each lead you get.

5. Time on site: how long do your customers stay on the website looking around? In the main the longer the better, but if they never get to the buy pages, it could indicate some challenges with your website.

People Measures

Your people are your greatest asset in the main, and so monitoring how they perform and how YOU perform with them is important. Measure:

1. Their efficiency. This may be orders completed or sales made per hour or calls taken. Whatever it is - measure it. And then set your team's objectives around those efficiencies.

2. Annual performance measures. Although you may think that your business is too small for this, it IS worth setting up annual or six-monthly appraisals from the beginning as it gets everyone in the habit of it. Set team and personal objectives tied to the business mission, objectives, targets or focus. Always have measures that relate to the key KPIs.

3. Staff costs: include here recruitment costs and all maintenance costs (wages, bonuses and support costs). You can then identify the staff cost per sale, for instance, and other profitability measures. Separate out the costs of your 'back office' i.e., non-productive or non-sales staff from the sales

teams whose costs should be included in the sales measures above.

4. Staff turnover: measure the frequency of staff losses and having to re-recruit. This change over of staff is a very costly part of any business and if you have a high staff turnover, there's something amiss – and it's likely to be you!

5. Salary or staff costs: keep these in line with industry averages.

6. Training days: give your teams an opportunity to develop and set them training targets. This will increase their personal satisfaction and will create a better workforce for your business.

Remember:

> CFO asks CEO: "What happens if we invest in developing our people and then they leave us?"
>
> CEO: "What happens if we don't, and they stay?"

7. Measure employee satisfaction: they won't always want to do this and you won't always want to receive it – but find a way to do this respectfully and confidentially: you will learn more than you expect, and it's a key piece of feedback for you as the business owner (after all you have no 'boss' to monitor you).

Financial Measures

Clearly you need to measure how well your business is doing and we're straying into the more formal reporting sections now, but examples for you to consider are:

1. Innovation or research and development spending: do you need to keep changing, upgrading or developing your product and if so, how much is that costing you? Do you need to add a few pence or cents to your current product prices to provide some money to keep this development going?

2. Debtor and creditor days taken: how quickly do you get paid and then how quickly do you have to pay suppliers? Ideally these two will match, and preferably you get paid before you have to pay suppliers, but keep a tight eye on this: don't let either of these payments get out of hand: cash flow is always managed better when it's tight and regular.

3. Fixed asset investment: do you have to buy equipment to run your business? How much is that going to cost, and how often does it need to be replaced? Do you need to add the cost of that to your current prices? How many sales can you get out of each piece of equipment? Can that productivity be improved?

4. Cost of borrowings and debt or overdrafts: don't forget to include any financing costs in your pricing.

5. Current ratio: this is a measure of your current assets (cash, stock, debtors etc) compared to your current liabilities (overdrafts, borrowings, suppliers

etc). Assets always need to be more than liabilities of course, but each business has different criteria here depending on all the issues and other measures above.

6. Revenue and profit by product, staff member, customer, outlet, distribution channel etc. Measure everything you can to find the strengths and weaknesses in your business.

And finally, (and we're now definitely into the formal reporting);

7. EBITDA: and this stands for Earnings before Interest, Taxation, Depreciation and Amortisation.

KPIs: Summary

Although there are many potential KPIs listed here, it is important that you keep these to a minimum otherwise they aren't KEY and you don't want to be measuring everything constantly as the numbers will lose their impact and effectiveness.

Start with a few Key KEY issues and then add measures as your business develops and you discover key areas to target. Only you will know what measures are right for your business, and each business will measure differently and in different ways. That doesn't matter. What matters is that you, as the business owner, understand what each measure is for and why it's important.

Remember, the idea with these is that you can sit away from the business and receive the information each day or week and understand and know exactly how the business is doing as a result. From that you need to know what to do, as the business leader, to keep it on track or to get it back on track quickly.

My top seven KPIs that I believe are relevant to any business are:

Top 7 KPIs: the KEY KPIs!

1. Cash
2. Sales
3. Profit (both gross and net) %
4. Customer acquisition cost
5. Sales per customer
6. Lead conversion, and
7. Customer feedback score

You also need to find an efficient way of collecting the information you need, and that brings us back to our **Management Information Systems** or MIS. There's no point in spending a fortune on collecting the data as all your profit will disappear, so MIS has to be simple, easy and clearly collected. If it is expensive to collect data you may not want to collect it all the time, it may be something you do only periodically.

Finally, you may not think you need KPIs – but YOU DO!!

It is very easy as a small business owner to feel that you know your business inside and out – and probably you do, but it is so easy to lose objectivity, especially when you're emotionally involved. Also, businesses change and what may have been right in the past may not be right for the future. Make sure you don't get left behind because of past assumptions and because you've always done it that way.

Finally, finally, MIS and KPIs are an important part of your automatic business process. If you decided never to come back from that beach in the Barbados how would your successors manage the business, what would they need to know? Make a note in your process manual of what KPIs are needed, what they tell you, and more importantly, what to do for a standard measure, a shortfall measure and an excess measure.

And enjoy that beach!

Now let's look at the formal reporting side of any business:

Part Two: Formal reporting

Business Reporting

When I started preparing this section of the book, my initial notes ran to pages and pages. Business reporting is a vast subject, so I have kept it to the initial and important issues that could land you in hot water so that, at the end of this section, you haven't nodded off and I haven't got repetitive strain injury!

This section of the book will feel different as business reporting is pretty black and white. My overarching top tip for you though is *get yourself a brilliant accountant*. I can't teach you everything you need to know in this section, but I can talk you through the main elements of business reporting. However, a brilliant accountant is a Godsend for any business and I urge you to find one that you can work with as they do very quickly become an integral part of your management team!

I have also added sections at the end where I share really useful links for you to use and which I know will help you with your business.

So which business structure should I use?

This is the most commonly asked question of accountants and is not always clear cut. It is important to lay the correct foundations so that your business can grow from an appropriate structure. Also, it's important that you review this periodically to adapt to the changing nature of your business.

What structure is right for me?

There is no right or wrong answer here but consider all the issues below! Professional advice should always be taken, but the key considerations are:

- Simplicity desired?
- Expected level of profits/losses?
- How many of you are involved?
- Do you need to limit personal liability?
- What is your tax position?
- Many others!

The important factors to consider overall are:

- Simplicity
- Will there be Income tax and national insurance on profits?
- Is Self-assessment reporting needed?
- How to create unlimited personal liability

We have covered the three most likely structures below:

1. Partnership

The important factors to consider are:

- It has more than one proprietor
- Simple to operate
- Income tax and national insurance is paid on profit share as earned
- Self-assessment reporting for partnership and partners
- Unlimited personal liability
- Joint and several liabilities (your creditors can pursue any individual partner personally for full debt)
- Legal agreement between partners is essential

2. Limited Liability Partnership

The important factors to consider for this structure are:

- Suitable for more than one proprietor
- It has more complex accounting requirements
- Income tax and national insurance are paid on profit share as earned (like a partnership)
- Self-assessment reporting is required for partnership and partners
- Accounts need to be filed at Companies House (publicly available) (like a company)
- It provides limited personal liability
- Legal agreement is required on formation

3. Limited Company

The important factors to consider for this structure are:

- Directors (run the company) and shareholders (control and own the company)
- It has more complex accounting requirements
- Corporation Tax is paid on profit as earned
- Income tax needs to be paid for Directors and Shareholders on profit taken from the company
- Can be useful to shelter income from higher rates of tax
- Accounts need to be filed at Companies House (publicly available)
- It provides limited personal liability
- It is a separate legal entity
- Articles of association are needed on formation

> **Useful links**
>
> https://www.peplows.co.uk/factsheets/starting-up-in-business
> https://www.gov.uk/government/publications/register-a-limited-liability-partnership-ll-in01
> https://www.gov.uk/limited-company-formation/register-your-company

Then What?!

Once you have your foundations in place, it is very tempting to forget the issue, but it's vital to diarize any legal reporting or regulatory requirements then you can get on with the fun stuff!

HRMC (Tax man!)

Sole Traders, Partnerships and Limited Liability Partnerships

These structures are subject to income tax and national insurance (class 2 and class 4) on profit as it is earned.

In order to register with HMRC you need a GOVERNMENT GATEWAY FIRST then file form SA1 online by 5 October following the end of the tax year in which your business started. Partnerships need to be registered separately.

N.B: The tax year runs from 6th April in any year to the 5th April the following year.

Ongoing obligations are then:

Tax Return filing

- By 31 January following the end of the tax year (31 October if filing a paper return)
- Penalties apply for late filing
- Returns can be amended for 12 months after the filing date and HMRC have 12 months in which to open an enquiry.

Paying your tax and national insurance

- On 31 January following the end of the tax year, generally based on the profits for the accounting year end falling in that tax year.
- Interest and Surcharges apply for late payment
- If your tax liability is >£1,000 you also have to pay 50% of that liability on account towards the following year on 31 January and 31 July – although you can apply to reduce this if you believe the following year's tax liability will be lower (penalties and interest can

apply for false/inaccurate claims).
- Be aware that your first payment may therefore be 150% of the tax, and "I've spent the money" will not be accepted as a reasonable excuse!

Bizarre excuses for late returns (that didn't wash)!
- My mother-in-law is a witch and put a curse on me
- I'm too short to reach the post box

- I was just too busy – my first maid left, my second maid stole from me, and my third maid was very slow to learn
- Our junior member of staff registered our client in Self-Assessment by mistake because they were not wearing their glasses
- My boiler had broken, and, my fingers were too cold to type

Limited Company

Companies are subject to corporation tax on profits at the rate shown in the useful links below.

You may register with HMRC at the same time that the company is formed. If not, you need a GOVERNMENT GATEWAY FIRST, then register online within 3 months of starting to do business.

Ongoing obligations are then:

Company Tax Return and accounts

- 12 months from accounting date (although see payment date below)
- Penalties apply for late filing
- Returns can be amended for 12 months after the filing date and HMRC have 12 months in which to open an enquiry.

Paying your tax

- 9 months from accounting date
- Interest applies
- Companies make payments on account only if their profits exceed £1,500,000 (split between associated companies).

When a new company is formed the accounting date is set to be the end of that month, but this can be changed if desired; as follows:

- Shortened
- Extended once every 5 years
- But any period cannot exceed 18 months.

Useful links

https://www.gov.uk/government-gateway
https://www.gov.uk/government/publications/self-assessment-register-for-self-assessment-and-get-a-tax-return-sa1
https://www.gov.uk/set-up-business-partnership/register-partnership-with-hmrc
https://www.gov.uk/limited-company-formation/set-up-your-company-for-corporation-tax
https://www.peplows.co.uk/resources/tax-rates-and-allowances
https://www.peplows.co.uk/resources/tax-calendar

Companies House

Now for Limited Companies and Limited Liability Partnership the ongoing filing requirements are:

- Accounts - within 9 months of the accounting date (watch date of first set)
- Confirmation statement (details of officers, shareholders/members (LLP) and persons of significant control) – annually
- Any changes to name, registered office, officers, shareholders/members (LLP) and persons of significant control, etc.

Failure to file can result in a fine or your company being struck off – in which case the assets pass to the crown! So, make sure you fully understand your obligations and make sure you surround yourself with the right experts to take any worry and fear away!

Now there have been many a bizarre excuse for late accounts (that also didn't wash)!

Some of the most outrageous reasons given include:

"Goats ate my accounts"

"I found my wife in the bath with my accountant"
"Pirates stole my accounts"

"We delivered the accounts to the betting office next door to Companies House"
"A volcano erupted and prevented me from filing"
"Slugs ate my accounts"
"It was Valentine's Day"
"My company was more successful than I thought it would be, so I was too busy to file"

Useful links

https://www.gov.uk/government/organisations/companies-house
https://www.gov.uk/government/news/people-with-significant-control-companies-house-register-goes-live

What are my Record Keeping obligations?

Groan, I know! But rather than seeing this as a necessary evil, consider how financial information will help you make informed business decisions and therefore aim to structure your records to add value to your KPI's.

Legal Requirement

- You must maintain adequate records to support the entries on tax return
- Failure will lead to a penalty of up to £3,000
- Such records must be kept for 5 years from 31 January following the tax year end for sole traders and partnerships
- For companies, the requirement is 6 years from the end of the accounting date.

Format

There is no prescribed format for keeping records, so could be:

- Manual (not shoe box of receipts!) – although see Making Tax Digital
- Excel spread sheets
- Software
- Cloud e.g. Xero, Sage, Quickbooks, or whatever
- What suits you best! Your accountant should be able to work with any, so it is more important for you to be comfortable using the system and to be able to obtain reports which help you in running your

business.
- Company Directors need to have accounting information sufficient to determine that they are not trading insolvently.

Making Tax Digital

Records will soon need to be kept in digital format – and already do for Vat returns. *Making Tax Digital* will introduce quarterly reporting for:

- VAT from April 2019 if vatable turnover > VAT limit - £85,000
- Corporation Tax currently delayed (but not cancelled!)
- Income Tax - self-employed businesses and landlords with business turnover > £10,000 from their next account period starting on or after 6 April 2024

Useful links

https://www.gov.uk/self-employed-records
https://www.gov.uk/government/publications/making-tax-digital/overview-of-making-tax-digital
https://www.xero.com/uk/signup/
https://uk.sageone.com/2013/11/06/why-try-before-you-buy/
https://tinyurl.com/y5xazgul
https://quickbooks.intuit.com/uk/accounting-software-free-trial/

Principles of Accounts preparation

"You must pay taxes. But there's no law that says you gotta leave a tip."–*Morgan Stanley advertisement*

Cash v Accruals basis

Accounts can be prepared on a cash basis if your turnover in the accounting period is <£150,000 and you must switch to the accruals basis if your turnover is >£300,000.

Accruals basis means income earned and expenses incurred during the period. If your business goes above the £150,000 limit in a tax year you can stay on the cash basis for that year then more onto accrual basis thereafter.

Cash means monies actually received and paid. This is simpler but can not be used by companies or LLPs.

Wholly and Exclusively

The tax rules state that expenditure cannot be deducted in computing trading profits unless it is <u>incurred wholly and exclusively for the purposes of the trade.</u>

Examples are, say, a parking fine which would not be allowable or excessive salary to a spouse or child.

In practice, HMRC will usually allow the business element of dual-purpose expenditure where it can reasonably be apportioned.

As well as unbelievable excuses, every year HMRC receive some dubious expenses claims for unconvincing items like woolly underwear and pet insurance for a dog. Some of the most questionable include:

- a carpenter claiming £900 for a 55-inch TV and sound bar to help him price his jobs
- £40 on extra woolly underwear, for 5 years
- £756 for my pet dog insurance
- a music subscription, so I can listen to music while I work
- a family holiday to Nigeria

All these excuses and expenses were unsuccessful. Not too surprising!

Capital v Revenue

Why does it matter?

- Revenue costs are allowable against profit in that year
- Capital costs are generally allowable against gains (which may come later) or given capital allowances if plant and machinery
- Day to day running costs are generally revenue
- Perpetual payments are generally revenue
- Payments for an enduring purpose are generally capital
- If the payment results in an asset, it is generally capital.

Pre trading expenditure

This is expenditure incurred before your trade starts. It is allowable if the trade started and is wholly and exclusively revenue in nature and incurred within the prior 7 years and it is treated as incurred on the first day of trading.

> **Useful links**
>
> https://www.gov.uk/hmrc-internal-manuals/business-income-manual

Issues particular to Limited Companies

Whilst Limited Companies offer a measure of limited liability and often the ability to mitigate your tax burden, they should not be entered into lightly! Accounts have to be prepared to specified formats, and there are more onerous regulatory requirements. There are some great targeted tax reliefs though, and it can also bring a certain gravitas to your business.

Formation tick list

- ✓ Try to ensure your company is formed with the correct SIC (Standard Industrial Classification) code
- ✓ As company information is publicly available, you may wish to have your Registered Office and Directors' Service Addresses at your accountants address rather than your home!
- ✓ You will need to choose Company Directors (who run the company) and Shareholders (who control and own the company) and the number of shares they hold.

✓ A Limited Company will also need its own bank account.

Company Directors

Being a director brings a number of duties and responsibilities:

- Duty to act within their powers
- Duty to promote the success of the company
- Duty to exercise independent judgement
- Duty to exercise reasonable care skill and diligence
- Duty to avoid conflicts of interest
- Duty not to accept benefits from third parties
- Duty to declare an interest in a proposed transaction or arrangement.

There is no longer a requirement to include a Company Secretary on formation.

IR35

This is tax legislation that is designed to combat tax avoidance by workers supplying their services to clients via an intermediary, such as a limited company, but who would be an employee if the intermediary was not used.

The main tests for these are:

- Control: what degree of control does the client have over what, how, when and where the worker completes the work?
- Substitution: is personal service by the worker

required, or can the worker send a substitute in their place?
- Mutuality of obligation**:** mutuality of obligation is a concept where the employer is obliged to offer work, and the worker is obligated to accept it.

If your contract is caught by IR35, you deduct your Pay As You Earn (PAYE) salary, a 5% expenses allowance, (but see below) plus any pension contributions. What is left must be treated as if it were a salary from an employer, so you calculate the additional tax due under PAYE. In effect, you have the disadvantage of being taxed as an employee with none of the employment rights.

Since April 2017 for contracts with the public sector, the responsibility for the deduction of PAYE rests with the engager. This also applies for all except small companies in the private sector with effect from April 2020.

- check employment status for tax www.gov.uk

SEIS (Seed Enterprise Investment Scheme)

If your start up requires investment, SEIS can be very attractive to investors. Benefits include:

- A 50% tax credit on up to £100,000 investment (in shares)
- Capital Gains Tax exemption on sale
- Deferral of other capital gains into the SEIS shares until sale
- If your trade is more than 2 years old, you could use EIS instead

R&D (Research and Development)

If your company is involved in innovation, it could get enhanced tax relief on certain expenditure it incurs for that purpose.

Separate Legal Entity

A limited company cannot be used as your personal piggy bank. Its assets are its own and in order to extract funds there are requirements which need to be followed. Lending funds to the company is fine and is generally by way of a Director's Loan. Borrowing money from your company can be done with shareholder approval but has tax consequences! If the loan is not repaid within 9 months of the accounting date, the company will face a 32.5% (potentially, 33.75% from April 2022) tax charge. In addition, if the loan is more than £10,000 the notional interest at the HMRC official rate (unless you actually pay it) is charged as a benefit in kind (see employment section below).

Remuneration Planning

Whilst every situation should be assessed, it is generally considered tax efficient to pay the maximum salary possible without paying national insurance (but still preserving state pension entitlement) and extracting the balance required as dividends. Please note that in order to pay a dividend, correct paperwork is required, and the company must have sufficient accumulated after-tax profits.

Interest

If a company pays interest to you (or a third party) as an individual and the loan is for more than 12 months, then it must deduct 20% basic rate income tax from the interest first and pay this over to HMRC quarterly 31 March, 30 June, 30 September and 31 December as well as reporting it on a form CT61 by the 14th of the following month. The recipient gets the net amount paid only.

Stationery

Limited companies have certain requirements as to the information required on its stationery:

Information required	Tick when completed						
	Letters	For goods / services orders	Invoices	Cheques	Official publications and forms	Premises
Name of company						
Country of registration						
Address of Registered Office						
Company number						
VAT number						
Forename or initial and surname						
(and nationality of non-EU directors) of ALL or NONE of the directors						

> **Useful links**
>
> https://www.gov.uk/government/publications/standard-industrial-classification-of-economic-activities-sic
> https://www.gov.uk/guidance/venture-capital-schemes-apply-to-use-the-seed-enterprise-investment-scheme
> https://www.gov.uk/guidance/venture-capital-schemes-apply-for-the-enterprise-investment-scheme
> https://www.gov.uk/guidance/corporation-tax-research-and-development-rd-relief
> https://www.gov.uk/government/publications/corporation-tax-return-of-income-tax-on-company-payments-ct61

What about Value Added Tax (VAT)?

On getting mugged: "I carry around months and months of receipts. I need a mugger who can file my VAT returns". Dara O'Brian

VAT is a vast subject in its own right, and a visit from the VAT inspector has been known to make even the most confident person's knees tremble.

Can I/should I register?

You can only register if making taxable supplies. So, ask yourself are your suppliers;

- Exempt (you cannot register)
- Zero rated (do not have to register)
- Reduce Rated
- Standard Rated

Registration can be either voluntary or compulsory. You can voluntarily register if you are making taxable supplies and registration can be especially useful if you provide zero rated supplies, where you charge VAT at 0% and can reclaim VAT on costs.

You are then registered then from the beginning of the following month.

Compulsory registration is required when <u>taxable supplies</u> exceed the threshold – currently £85,000 in a rolling period of 12 months, or you buy such a VAT registered business as a going concern.

When the threshold is exceeded, you need to register by the end of the following month to apply from the first of the month after that. Compulsory registration also applies if taxable turnover is expected to exceed the threshold in the next 30 days alone.

If you take over an existing VAT registered business as a going concern, you will need to carry on the vendor's 12 month rolling calculations.

In order to register, you need a GOVERNMENT GATEWAY FIRST.

Then register online with HMRC. Sign up to Making Tax Digital if your turnover exceeds the registration threshold.

Once registered, requirements are:

Invoices

These details must be included on a VAT invoice:

- Number and time of supply/date of issue
- Name and address of you and customer
- Your VAT number
- Description of goods and cost

- Rate and amount of VAT charged
- Discount, if any
- Reason for any zero rating

VAT Returns

- Would normally be submitted quarterly but can be monthly (if regular VAT refunds) or annual (if scheme applied for).

Normal Rules

- Returns are generally quarterly (you can change quarter dates)
- Output VAT (charged by you) is payable to HMRC
- Minus any VAT incurred for business purposes
- Special rules for cars, entertainment, gifts, etc
- Partial exemption – you may not be able to recover all input VAT if you make some exempt supplies.

Flat rate scheme

If you apply to join the flat rate scheme:

- Choose the rate for your business (1% discount for first year)
- You pay 16.5% if limited cost trader (<2% turnover spent on goods)
- you still charge full VAT to customers
- Pay the reduced rate on VAT inclusive sales
- No claim for VAT on costs
- There is less administration required
- Cash accounting – pay on receipt and payment not

on invoice
- You can still apply for other schemes if you meet the criteria.
- Annual accounting – yearly VAT return with payments on account
- There are other schemes which may apply such as: Margin scheme – second-hand goods, VAT paid on margin (sale less direct cost)
Gold scheme
Retail schemes

Useful links

https://www.gov.uk/government-gateway
https://www.gov.uk/vat-registration/how-to-register
https://www.gov.uk/guidance/sign-up-for-making-tax-digital-for-vat
https://www.gov.uk/vat-flat-rate-scheme/how-much-you-pay
https://www.gov.uk/government/collections/vat-manuals
https://www.gov.uk/hmrc-internal-manuals/vat-flat-rate-scheme
https://www.gov.uk/vat-businesses
https://www.gov.uk/vat-record-keeping/vat-invoices
https://www.gov.uk/guidance/rates-of-vat-on-different-goods-and-services

Becoming an employer!

If you ask business owners, most will say that employing staff is their biggest challenge, but it is also vital to the success and growth of your business.

'It is not the employer who pays the wages. Employers only handle the money. It is the customer who pays the wages.' Henry Ford

It is also the employer that collects the tax and national insurance (and now pension) on behalf of HMRC!

In the first instance, you need to register with HMRC as an employer.

GOVERNMENT GATEWAY FIRST

- Then register as an employer
- If you take over an existing business, the staff will transfer under Transfer of Undertakings (protection of employment) regulations along with their employment rights
- When paying employees, you must operate Pay As You Earn (income tax, employers and employees) national insurance and report to HMRC under Real Time Information. You can use HMRC basic tools for up to 5 employees (free!) or third-party software.
- Employees should provide P45 or a P46
- You are responsible for operating the correct tax code
- Pay and deductions paid for month ended on 5th of each month to be paid to HMRC by 19th.

Penalties apply

Most employers will be entitled to the annual employment allowance which exempts the first £4,000 of employers' national insurance. Also, no employer's national insurance will generally be due in respect of employees under 21 and apprentices under 25.

You are also required to operate Statutory Sick, Maternity and Paternity Pay (where employees qualify) and provide at least statutory annual leave, as follows:

- Sick pay entitlement after required waiting days
- Maternity pay and leave entitlement – if your employee qualifies,
- Paid annual leave of 5.6 weeks (incl. bank hols), even if on sick or maternity leave.

Company Directors

- National Insurance is paid on a cumulative basis like tax
- With a salary up to £9,100 per annum (2022/23) there is no national insurance but state pension entitlement is preserved – a win win!
- Minimum wage and auto enrolment (below) do not apply if there is no contract of employment.

Minimum Wage

You must pay your employees at least the minimum wage and keep sufficient records to prove this.

Currently hourly rates

Apprentice	£4.81
<18	£4.81
18-20	£6.83
21-22	£9.18
23 and over	£9.50

Penalties apply for non-compliance – between 100% and 200% of underpayment!

Auto Enrolment

As an employer you may now have to provide a workplace pension which involves minimum contributions by the employee and employer, if an employee is:

Between 22 – state pension age

Earning >£10,000 per annum

An employee can opt out but have to go in first and you cannot encourage them to do so!

Benefits in kind

If you provide non-cash benefits to your employees (or you as a Director) you need to report these annually on a form P11d by 6 July following the tax year. Your employee is then taxed on the benefit and the employer pays 13.8% (15.05% from April 2022) national insurance.

The most common taxable benefits are:
- Car
- Fuel
- Private Medical

- Accommodation
- Reduced or interest-free loans

Employment Related Securities

If a past, present or future employee or a Director acquires shares in their employers' company, then a form 42 may need to be filed by 6 July following the tax year.

If the shares are acquired at less than market value, then income tax (and more rarely national insurance) may be due.

Other issues to consider:

- Right to work in UK
- Employers liability insurance
- Health and safety
- Discrimination
- Redundancy procedures
- Data protection
- And many more!

Construction Industry Scheme

If your business is in the Construction industry and you use sub-contractors, you will also be required to operate CIS.

You need to initially verify the subcontractor (whether a sole trader, partnership or a company) online and HMRC will advise if you need to withhold tax from the payment to them and at what rate. You pay that tax to

HMRC by 19th following the tax month ending on the 5th.

If a payment is for goods and labour, you can exclude the goods element at cost only.

There are heavy penalties for non-compliance, be warned!

Useful links

https://www.gov.uk/government-gateway
https://www.gov.uk/register-employer
https://www.gov.uk/topic/business-tax/payehttps://www.gov.uk/new-employee/employee-information
https://www.gov.uk/statutory-sick-pay
https://www.gov.uk/government/publications/construction-industry-scheme-cis-340/construction-industry-scheme-a-guide-for-contractors-and-subcontractors-cis-340
https://www.gov.uk/holiday-entitlement-rights
https://www.gov.uk/national-minimum-wage
https://www.gov.uk/workplace-pensions
https://www.gov.uk/employer-reporting-expenses-benefits
https://www.gov.uk/topic/business-tax/employment-related-securities
https://www.gov.uk/maternity-pay-leave/pay

With reporting, tax and finances a DIY approach is usually dangerous, so professional advice is recommended.

LEADERSHIP

Introduction

Leadership has many facets and forms, and although most people would identify leadership as **people** leadership, I also want to cover business leadership as well.

A. Leading the people: Introduction

Leadership is a relatively modern phenomenon, and it certainly isn't what I experienced when I first started in business 40 years ago.

Business used to be more hierarchical: there was possibly a director, then a manager and then a supervisor, and then the team. Nowadays business structures are flatter and are more linear: the boss is no longer the feared presence they once were. Business teams are empowered to do their own thinking rather than waiting for an instruction from on high.

And that makes sense because business is different. Teams today have to be prepared to deal with the ordinary and the extraordinary and to make decisions within a frame work because a decision is needed fast or the customer goes and the business has been left behind.

To be a good leader today, you need two things: the tangible facts on how to drive the business forward together with the intangible emotional power to motivate. (If you recognise the two sides of the Scales of Abundance, then reward yourself with a treat). The emotional side was rarely recognised 40 years ago,

There are lots of definitions of leadership, but I think the best one is:

The ability to engage the hearts and minds of the workforce in pursuit of a common goal.

The Minds

This is an intellectual exercise and involves getting the workforce engaged mentally with the mission, objectives and targets of the business. It follows that all these areas must be crystal clear to all and well communicated by the leader.

However, once the mission is established and the team 'get' what the business is about, they can contribute to team objectives and targets themselves and this helps to get them engaged emotionally with their work.

The Hearts

A leader can only gain the heart of an employee after a lot of hard work. The employee needs to believe in the business and believe in you as a leader, and this belief would have been generated over time through mutual trust and respect. The team member needs to be emotionally involved and keen to be a part of the business.

When you have fully captured the hearts and the minds of a team member, then you have a disciple – one who would follow you anywhere and probably do the work for free. That is rare!

As well as leadership now being recognised as a combination of art and science today, there are different kinds of leadership such as coaching leadership, environmental leadership, group leadership and so on. It's a very broad topic, but for now we'll look at what a leader looks like.

'If your actions inspire others to dream more, learn more, do more and become more, you are a leader.'-
John Quincy Adams, 6th President of the United States

Characteristics of a great leader

A leader has to be a superhero and I can confirm I don't know anyone who has all these characteristics listed below, but let's start with the perfect leader and go from there:

1. Self-awareness. Before anyone can even hope to inspire or lead another individual, they need to understand whether they have the skill set or not. It's perfectly understandable for a business owner to think that they may be the best person to lead the organisation, but in many cases the passion they have for their product or service is just not enough to lead others. There's also the issue that if you are so passionate about your product, you may not be able to see the challenges and weaknesses that your team is aware of, consequently you won't be able to

lead them anywhere.

It is a very self-aware person who understands that they may not be the best man or woman for the job and if that is the case, they need to find a business leader who will absorb the passion and convert it into team activity.

Not everyone is a natural leader and although many of these skills can be acquired, the truly great leaders have an aptitude and a natural instinct for leadership.

2. Bravery. It is a very brave person to lead a team into difficult circumstances. There is a military analogy about burning the bridges that come from an army marching forward and then burning the bridges (their escape route in the case of retreat) behind them. We can see that having burnt their bridges this army has no other course of action but to go forward, and that understanding must make them more determined to succeed.

   However, to be able to make that all-or-nothing decision in business is tough, and although hopefully no one will get physically hurt if such a decision is made it can be incredibly damaging to the business and team morale if the decision or result in action doesn't work.

   Also, these extreme all or nothing decisions cannot be made too often because the team will become desensitised to it and the impact will be lost.

   It is a very brave leader who is capable of making extreme decisions and a very brave leader who decides not to.

Furthermore, a good business leader needs to be brave enough to go out on a limb and to go to places previously unexplored and to take their team with them. The business will only be truly successful if it eventually moves into uncharted territory otherwise it becomes static and stale. If the business leader can do this, the team will find it exciting and motivating.

3. Belief. A strong business leader needs belief in three things:

    - The business product or service, its mission, purpose and objectives.
    - Themselves and their ability to lead the team and to communicate the business messages with total conviction and belief.
    - The team and their ability to implement the mission.

4. Very strong personnel skills. No team member ever improved their performance by being moaned at but sometimes corrective feedback has to be given and it's how this is done that differentiates a good leader from a bad one. Team members have to feel empowered, supported and engaged, and if they are slightly hesitant about communicating honestly and openly to their leader, they will always be holding something back and won't be performing at their best.

5. Integrity. A strong leader has to walk the walk, talk the talk, dream the dream with no doubt or hesitation. If the leader has even a speck of doubt regarding anything they want the team to do, then the team will intuitively feel that and again they hold

something back with their performance.

I remember a silly quote from my university days: "I have all the skills I need for this job except integrity and as soon as I learn to fake that I'll be fine".
Clearly that won't work.

Integrity also goes alongside the personnel skills, as each team member needs to feel that they are being communicated with in a safe way. If a team leader gossips or moans about one team member to another that becomes very damaging as the team member hearing the gossip or moan will then understand that they could be in the firing line and the team leader might gossip about them to somebody else. This takes trust out of the relationship.

6. Trust. This underlines many of the other characteristics and goes hand-in-hand with other skills. A strong leader needs to be able to trust that the team will do their best and needs to place themselves in a position where the team knows without any doubt that they can put their unequivocal trust in the leader.

7. Delegation. An aware business leader knows that their role is to lead and not necessarily to do. A business leader needs to understand their team and their respective strengths and weaknesses, such that they can place the best person in each individual role or task for the benefit of the group whole.

Delegation in itself is an art form, and a leader needs to understand how to give clear and precise directions and parameters for each task in hand as well as to pass on both the rights and responsibilities of the job. It is too common that delegation involves passing on the responsibilities without the rights that would enable the team member to perform, and at that stage they are doomed for failure.

8. Inspiration and motivation. This is a really difficult characteristic to debate. Most people would recognise that some human beings just have the ability to encourage and inspire others, whereas lesser immortals find this difficult. However, I do not believe that inspirational leaders are born and not made and everyone can make a huge impact on their motivational or inspirational abilities should they choose to.

Firstly, my view is that inspiration or motivation springs initially from enthusiasm. If a leader is enthusiastic about their role, the business and the team, then that is the first huge step taken. Nothing spreads faster than enthusiasm and a business leader should have enthusiasm for the business or product otherwise they're doing the wrong thing.

However, enthusiasm isn't enough on its own and motivation comes from adding belief, integrity and all the other characteristics on top.

Although clearly it is hugely beneficial as a leader if you have oratory skills, but they are rare. Inspiration and motivation can come from the actions you take, and not necessarily from the big rousing speeches that we all wish we could make.

As a business leader I learnt early on that getting stuck into a task was motivational to my team. The fact that I was prepared to do what some would consider being menial tasks meant that others were more prepared to follow.

I'm not suggesting that every business leader needs to be making the tea or doing photocopying, but my belief is that a strong leader has the ability and enthusiasm to do these tasks should the situation arise. There is nothing more motivational than seeing the boss or team leader mucking in and doing one of those essential menial tasks in pursuit of business excellence. It also places the business leader quite firmly within the team itself rather than at a distance and creates a very strong team bond.

If you sit within a team stuffing envelopes, for example you very quickly become part of that team working towards a common goal and objective and that will motivate everybody.

It also places the team leader into a democracy, which recognises every team member is equal. Most team members would appreciate that and find it motivational.

In addition, most team members would be motivated by the fact that they are respected and their voice is heard. Please take time to really listen to what your team is saying, even if it's not necessarily what you want to hear. A team member needs to feel secure enough with you as a business leader to trust that their opinion is respected and heard, and that will give them confidence and will inspire them to do their best.

9. Decision-making. The business leader needs to be capable of making a clear business decision and communicating that effectively. If the message lacks focus or is anyway unclear, the team will not move forward appropriately. What team members want is complete clarity on what is expected of them and the outcome they are expected to achieve otherwise they hesitate and all is lost.

   What may be painfully obvious to you as the business leader, and possibly business owner, is not painfully obvious to anyone else and the more I am in business the more I realise that communication needs to come down to the lowest common denominator. You can make sure that your communication is clear either by testing it on one team member ahead of the others or by providing a safe environment where the team can ask questions without fear of recriminations. The team will only communicate as effectively as you have communicated to them, and if they are not fulfilling what you believe you have asked them to do, then that's your fault!

   Decisions need to be well communicated and relatively fast. If a team member has an issue, then they won't really focus on any of the tasks in their remit if they are waiting for clarity on one particular item. Also, if one team member has an issue, then it's almost certain that the others have the same issue; they may not just have flagged it to you yet.

Be honest and clear with your team if a decision needs to be made and you cannot make it immediately. In many cases it will simply be a matter of clarity and you can decide and communicate by return. If you need to go away and check facts and figures, then say so and give them an appropriate timescale for your response.

If you need to check a decision with a business owner or board of directors which would take longer, then again say so but chase up your superiors with energy. Your team will respect you for that, as they will feel that you are fighting their corner and you're on their side.

10. The desire to increase the abilities of the team and to develop relationships within it. A good business leader is self-less and puts the team before themselves. There is a famous quote that says that business leaders eat last and although I probably believe that the team should all eat together, I do understand this act of selflessness and putting the team first. A business leader should genuinely care for their team and the individuals within it and want them to improve and connect and be the best that they can be within your organisation. This doesn't mean you have to like everybody as clearly that isn't possible, but a good business leader recognises the strength of even those people they don't like and positively attempts to utilise their skills for the common good.

This is a very important part of the leader's skill set. An inexperienced team leader will pull together a team of people they like and feel that are easy to lead. This is one strategy, but eventually a good business leader appreciates some skills that they don't necessarily have come from people they don't necessarily like.

Most naïve business leaders would select a team of people that were just like themselves and clearly that is inefficient. I remember acknowledging to myself that I had moved up a level when I recruited somebody that wasn't like me and I genuinely didn't take to, but I felt she had the right skill set for the job. She proved me right, and she was very good at her role, but I don't think she and I ever gelled as people. That doesn't really matter because over time we developed a huge respect for each other's skills.

You need to choose your team based on the tasks in hand and the skill sets needed meanwhile always having an eye open for increasing the skills, and increasing the talents of the people at your disposal. You need to have a positive and clear enhancement and training programme for all of your team members, as it will make them feel valued and ultimately will be better for the business.

I remember the quote that says: "what if I train my people and they then leave" to which the answer is "what if you don't train them and they stay". I've always preferred training and encouraging staff, and this has produced dividends for me over my business life. I have had many occasions where staff member has left our organisation in pursuit of something better, only to return a few months later acknowledging that what they had with us was difficult to replicate. People will always be loyal to you, even if they leave the business temporarily, if you treat them well and even if they never come back to the business, you will still have an advocate out there in the wider world who will speak well of you as a business leader and as an organisation.

I'm a firm believer in the fact that I'm not good at everything and understand that for most tasks there will be somebody much better qualified and able to do a task than me. This connects very well with the self-awareness characteristic that we had earlier. The sooner you understand what your own skills are and what your role might be, the better. Once you understand that recruit team members that fill in all the gaps.

In the main there will always be somebody better than you to do any task, and the sooner your ego accepts that the better.

In my role within the Chamber of Commerce I will occasionally go to businesses to give them some mentoring or guidance and it is very common for a business owner to believe that they are the only person that can do any of the tasks and eventually that will drag them down and the business will fail. Although it may be acceptable for a small business owner to undertake tasks initially, the quicker they start to distance themselves and involve other people, the greater the chance that their business will be successful.

Many people come from the position that it is easier to do a task themselves than to attempt to train someone else to do it. Initially, this is true, but sooner or later the task will have to be done elsewhere.

No small business owner should give up work and give up working 40 hours a week for an idiot who is their boss, to work more than 40 hours a week for an even bigger idiot in themselves.

11. Honesty. Most of the other skills listed here involve honesty somewhere: to yourself, to the business and to the team, but it's worth mentioning it as a separate characteristic such that it doesn't get forgotten.

    A business leader needs to be honest with and about themselves, about the business and about the team, otherwise they can't lead.

Summary

Looking at that long list of characteristics it seems that leadership is almost an impossible task, but given good training and development most people can grow into being a good leader.

But it isn't easy, and great leaders are very few and far between.

In the beginnings of any business, it is usually the business owner that by default becomes the business leader and that will work reasonably well in the short term. The business owner has the belief and the passion about the product or service, and this will be enough to carry the team through as it grows and develops.

But like the processing chapter we had before, eventually the business owner needs to let go and let somebody else lead the business whilst they, the business owner work on moving the business up the tiers of the pyramid rather than being an integral part of doing the business itself.

Leadership is a career to be taken very seriously. It needs practice, qualifications, and experience to do it well. There are many fantastic leadership programs available nowadays and so there is no excuse for being a bad leader. Although it may be helpful to have some natural leadership talents, it isn't essential and many people can acquire the skills over time.

B. Business leadership

Whether you, as the business owner, become the leader of the people within it – or not – you will always remain the leader of the business itself. As the ultimate person in the business, you need to decide on where it's going and lead it there.

What you need is:

1. A business vision. This is where all businesses start – in the mind's eye of the owner. It doesn't matter if the business starts from a redundancy or frustration or a lifelong dream, every business owner or business starter normally has a dream of what the business could be.

    That vision or dream will normally change over time, and as the business grows or develops up the tiers of the pyramid.

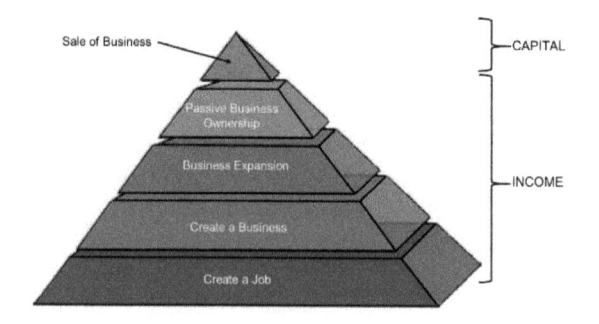

Pyramid diagram (bottom to top): Create a Job, Create a Business, Business Expansion, Passive Business Ownership, Sale of Business. The bottom four tiers are bracketed as INCOME; the top tier is bracketed as CAPITAL.

For some, the vision will never change. If the aim of the business is to create yourself a job (Tier One) and you do that, then there is no future vision or need for leadership – unless your business aim changes.

However, if you begin there but then start to develop an objective to move up the pyramid and decide to create, and expand a business, then the vision changes.

Or it could be that you start the business with the end in mind to create franchises or to sell it, and you have a clear vision of that from the off. If you do, make that vision as vivid and clear as you can and then spend your time making that vision a reality.

2. Once you have your vision clear, you need to make that clear to others, and that usually involves creating a business and a strategic plan. This is normally so that you can share your vision with a fund provider who will want to understand what your vision is, and where the business is going before they lend you any money.

Although these two plans are often used synonymously, one covers the longer-term vision and one covers the shorter term future, although frankly, it doesn't really matter as long as you are clear and you cover all the points below.

Your aim is to lead the business into the future and into success.

Strategic Plan

A strategic plan should clarify the mid to long term goals and vision covering the next 5 – 10 years and should cover:

- An executive summary identifying the vision, mission, and ultimate expectations of where the business is going. The pyramid may help to identify that ultimate purpose,
- a summary of the product or service
- the values of the business and a sense of the position of the business in the market place
- a summary of financials and other measurements such as potential market share. The financials should cover, as a minimum, overall sales and profitability. As a suggestion here, most fund providers like to see a sustained and regular growth, even if the business makes a loss in the first year or so. It's also useful to have more than one measure of the financials; such as best or worse case scenarios,
- the main objectives of the business needed in order to bring the vision into reality, and
- an indication of perspective and your awareness of the external world, and where your own business fits within it: a SWOT analysis is ideal for this identifying the Strengths, Weaknesses, Opportunities, and Threats of the business.

Strengths	Weaknesses
Opportunities	Threats

SWOT Analysis Template

A strategic plan need not be overly long or intimidating.

Business Plan

A business plan takes the strategic plan and vision and demonstrates how you intend to turn that into reality. A business plan normally covers the next year or so and will include:

- An indication of yearly financial progress in more detail than the overview in the strategic plan such as sales, cost of sales, overheads and gross and net profitability. You may also include product pricing information and other financials as relevant to your particular business.
- Specific goals and objectives by department or business section (which you then feed down to your department heads or leaders),

    My view is that these plans need to be as close to your reality as you can make them – then they are useful documents. It saddens me that many entrepreneurs create these plans and then file them away as if they are an independent and irrelevant exercise.

Done appropriately, the strategic and business plans provide the framework for leading the business to success.

Finally, as well as these big picture documents, the other tools available to a leader of a business are the Key Performance Indicators as they provide tactical guidance on a weekly or monthly basis. See the reporting section for more information there.

'Perfection is not attainable. But if we chase perfection, we can catch excellence.'- **Vince Lombardi**

FINISHING BLOCKS

Business summary

Business is a dynamic thing: it doesn't stay still or if it does, the market and the customer changes so something is always on the move. In those circumstances it's quite difficult to write a comprehensive guide to business book, especially as every business is different.

What I've aimed to do here is to provide a pick and mix buffet style of information for you to dip in and out of. Sales and Marketing has made up the biggest slice of the book because that's the area that most people struggle with and the area that I get most questions about.

I'm also conscious that if you're running your own business, you don't have much spare time to go on courses or to educate yourself, but you do need information on a needs basis as you progress. Hopefully, you will find that information here.

I've also concentrated on the bottom tiers of the pyramid, as that's where most small businesses sit either through choice or circumstance. Hopefully, we may have encouraged some of you to move up the pyramid a little to something bigger and more successful.

This pyramid or hierarchical approach to business is about taking a business idea or taking YOU and your skill set and growing it organically from the bottom up, and whether you intend to stay at the bottom Tier or move on up to Tier Five, always start with the end in mind and approach that business AS IF you could sell it one day as that gives you the right perspective on how to set that business up more strategically in the first place. By doing that you create an asset of some kind, that can create a capital gain or some income in the future either for you or your descendants. Think big picture and big money, and it doesn't do to sell yourself short or to minimise your time or impact.

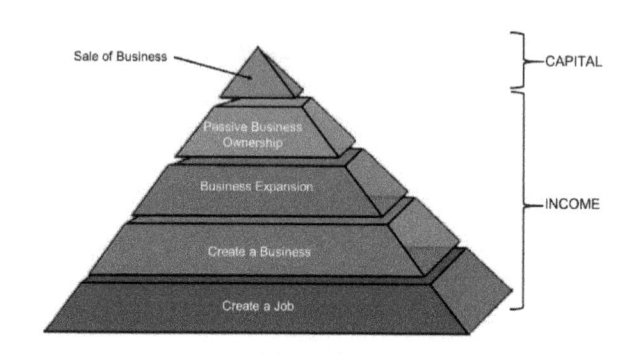

[Pyramid diagram: from top to bottom — Sale of Business (CAPITAL); Passive Business Ownership, Business Expansion, Create a Business, Create a Job (INCOME)]

However, if this is too dull for you and you can't wait to grow a business organically, then you can be a business buyer and seller and start picking up businesses from say Tier Two or Three and give them your magic systemising sparkle and sell them on as a Tier Four or Five. That's just like doing a property Capital Project and refurbishing a run-down house.

Or you could just buy franchises and buy a ready-made business that someone else has created. That's good for income – for you and for the franchisor - but there's no capital gain there for you.

Your life – your wealth – your choice.

As before, there are many topics that we don't have space to cover here such as business planning, selection of business area and choosing a niche: business targeting and focus, fund raising, impacts of the external economy and so on.

There is nothing so satisfying as seeing your business

dream become a reality and for a lucky few, including me, the business is much more than that.

Fielding Financial is my main business, and it is the embodiment of my life purpose, my mission and of course, it is my life legacy. To see it as it now is with hundreds of people working on that mission is incredibly humbling and overwhelming.

I'd swap any job for that any day and for me, my business allows me to be me: it gives me a sense of liberation and huge satisfaction.

They are not the normal, or expected outcomes from a business, I know that, but I can only wish you the same feelings.

I wish you health, wealth and happiness.

Appendix

The whacky world of marketing acronyms

B2B: Business to Business – Marketing preformed between businesses

B2C – Business to Consumer – Marketing from a business directly to a customer.

BR: Bounce Rate - Refers to how long a customer stays on your website page, whether they stayed to read or book or whether they left straight away having clicked through. BR also refers to emails and whether an email has reached the intendeds inbox or bounced back to the sender.

CMS: Content Management System – A tool whereby you can schedule and analyse your digital marketing efforts.

CPC: Cost Per Click – Method used to charge for ad space on a website. Businesses advertising only pay for the ad when it's been clicked, not how often it's been seen.

CPL: Cost Per Lead – Considers all the costs that go into generating a lead.

CPM: Cost Per Thousand – Method of charging for advertising. It counts how many times the ad has been seen, not how many times it's been clicked.

CRM: Customer Relationship Management – A software platform that allows a business to manage and analyse their database. Designed to help convert leads, nurture sales, and retain customers.

CTA: Call to Action – Can be a copy, a link button or image and it instructs the user/ customer to do something / take action.

CTR: Click Through Rate – Refers to the amount of people who have completed an action for example click a button on your website or within an email campaign.

CR: Conversion Rate - **The number of people who act, divided by the number that could have. You can find this metrics within Google Analytics.**

GA: Google Analytics – **Google Analytics is a tool that helps marketers better understand their audience, reach, activity, and metrics.**

HTML: Hypertext Markup Language - **HTML is a set of 'rules' programmers used to create web pages. It describes the content, structure, text, images and objects used on a webpage. Today, most websites run HTML in the background.**

KPI: Key Performance Indicators – Used to track performance of marketing efforts.

PPC: Pay Per Click - **A publisher who charges advertisers for each action taken (click) on their ad. See CPC as well.**

SEO: Search Engine Optimisation - Purpose is to help your content 'get found' on the internet. The process allows your website to become highly searchable within search engines.

SM: Social Media – Platforms include **Facebook, LinkedIn, Twitter, Instagram and Pinterest. These can be used for personal accounts or business accounts.**

SMB: Small and Medium-Sized Businesses – Describes a business with between 5-200M in revenue and companies with 100 or fewer employees.

SMART: Specific, Measurable, Attainable, Realistic, Time-Bound - **Used to define the goal-setting process.**

SMM: Social Media Marketing – Used to promote a business

Contributors

Thank you to Debbie Franklin, Lara Carter and Louise Thorpe.
Stories from Gill Fielding, Erzsebet Kohut, Ainsley John, Natasha Scott www.scottinventories.co.uk, Martin Edgar.